SEA-MARK
The Metaphorical Voyage,
Spenser to Milton

LIVERPOOL ENGLISH TEXTS AND STUDIES
General editors: JONATHAN BATE and BERNARD BEATTY

This long-established series has a primary emphasis on close reading, critical exegesis and textual scholarship. Studies of a wide range of works are included, although the list has particular strengths in the Renaissance, and in Romanticism and its continuations.

Byron and the Limits of Fiction edited by Bernard Beatty and Vincent Newey. Volume 22. 1988. 304pp. ISBN 0–85323–026–9

Literature and Nationalism edited by Vincent Newey and Ann Thompson. Volume 23. 1991. 296pp. ISBN 0–85323–057–9

Reading Rochester edited by Edward Burns. Volume 24. 1995. 240pp. ISBN 0–85323–038–2 (cased), 0–85323–309–8 (paper)

Thomas Gray: Contemporary Essays edited by W. B. Hutchings and William Ruddick. Volume 25. 1993. 287pp. ISBN 0–85323–268–7

Nearly Too Much: The Poetry of J. H. Prynne by N. H. Reeve and Richard Kerridge. Volume 26. 1995. 224pp. ISBN 0–85323–840–5 (cased), 0–85323–850–2 (paper)

A Quest for Home: Reading Robert Southey by Christopher J. P. Smith. Volume 27. 1997. 256pp. ISBN 0–85323–511–2 (cased), 0–85323–521–X (paper)

Outcasts from Eden: Ideas of Landscape in British Poetry since 1945 by Edward Picot. Volume 28. 1997. 344pp. 0–85323 531–7 (cased), 0–85323–541–4 (paper)

The Plays of Lord Byron, edited by Robert F. Gleckner and Bernard Beatty. Volume 29. 1997. 400pp. 0–85323–881–2 (cased), 0–85323–891–X (paper)

SEA-MARK

The Metaphorical Voyage, Spenser to Milton

PHILIP EDWARDS

LIVERPOOL UNIVERSITY PRESS

First published 1997 by
LIVERPOOL UNIVERSITY PRESS
Senate House, Abercromby Square, Liverpool, L69 3BX

British Library Cataloguing-in-Publication Data
A British Library CIP Record is available for this book

ISBN 0–85323–512–0 *cased*
      0–85323–522–8 *paper*

Set in Linotron 202 Garamond by
Wilmaset Limited, Birkenhead, Wirral
Printed and bound in the European Union by
Page Brothers, Norwich

Contents

PREFACE

I am grateful to a number of friends who have helped my work on this book at various stages, particularly Bernard Beatty, Nick Davis, Howard Erskine-Hill, Nicholas Grene, Geoffrey Holloway, Ernst Honigmann, Molly Mahood and Michael Screech. I am also grateful to Seiko Aoyama, Manfred Draudt, Tetsuo Kishi and Holger Klein for allowing me to discuss my ideas on *Othello* with their colleagues and students in Japan and Austria.

I have not modernized the spelling in my quotations (except for the forms of the letters u, v, j). If some readers find the original spelling awkward, even difficult, I am sorry. But modern spelling may give a false sense of familiarity to authors of the distant past. Much of the argument in *Sea-Mark* depends on a detailed teasing out of the meaning of passages, and modern spelling, making the authors seem much nearer to us than they actually are, sometimes suggests a misleading modern meaning. Old spelling operates a bit like Brecht's *Verfremdung*. It creates a space between us and the text, and in the end brings it nearer to us by keeping it at a distance in the first place. In maintaining the original spelling of my texts, there is not often much hope of preserving the author's actual spelling, but at least the text appears in a form with which the author would have felt at home.

There is obviously a problem about Shakespeare: two problems in fact. The first is that we are so accustomed to reading Shakespeare in modern spelling; the second is what 'original spelling' means when the accepted text comes as so often from more than one source. For the first problem, I can only repeat what I have said; it is no bad thing to be de-familiarized. For the second problem, there was little question that for the plays I deal with the Folio of 1623 was the ideal text. It is the only source of the texts of *Macbeth*, *The*

Tempest, *The Comedy of Errors*, and *The Winter's Tale*. It is by far the best text for *Othello*. *The Merchant of Venice* and *A Midsummer Night's Dream* present no real problem in the passages I quote, and any variants from the quartos are noted. For *Pericles* there is only a quarto text, of very poor quality, and that has been used with the necessary editing. In quotations from all authors, significant editing is noted, but occasionally minor changes have been made silently.

Some material from Chapter One (on Spenser) and Chapter Six (on Shakespeare) appears in an essay, 'The Rapture of the Sea', to be published in *Shakespearean Continuities*, ed. J. Batchelor, T. Cain, and C. Lamont (Macmillan).

The 'sea-mark' of my title comes from the *Othello* passage which is the centre of my discussion of the play. The phrase also comes into *The Faerie Queene*—referring to the white cliffs of Dover. It meant a prominent object acting as a guide to mariners, but Othello used it ironically, to denote a false or mistaken aim. I chose it for my title because one of my main themes is the duplicity of what is perhaps the most prominent of all literary metaphors, the metaphor of the voyage.

Kendal, Cumbria, 1996

ACKNOWLEDGEMENT

Quotations from Oxford editions cited in Chapters 1, 2, 3 and 8 are made by kind permission of Oxford University Press. The sources are given in footnotes to the text.

INTRODUCTION

This book is a comparative study of the use made by six
writers of the sixteenth and seventeenth centuries—Spenser,
Marlowe, Donne, Shakespeare, Bacon, Milton—of the
traditional metaphor of the voyage, perhaps the commonest
metaphor in literature, going back beyond Horace, who
warned the battered ship of state not to venture out into
stormy seas (Odes, I, xiv), and going on beyond Hardy's
'Convergence of the Twain', which made the loss of the
Titanic a symbol of the workings of the Immanent Will. It
seems to me that in the period I am concerned with the
metaphor had, in the work of some writers at least, a special
vitality, and that new energy and meaning were injected into
convention and cliché. It is obvious that there ought to be
some connection between this vitality and the fast-increasing
activities of English ships at sea during this time: the voyages
of discovery, trading voyages, expeditions against Spain and
her shipping, voyages to create settlements in the New World.
The year 1588 saw the defeat of the Armada and the
triumphant retrurn of Thomas Cavendish from his voyage
round the world, and in the following year Richard Hakluyt
published the first version of his *Principall Navigations,
Voiages, and Discoveries of the English Nation*. It is hard to
think that the imagination of a writer in England at this time
would not take some tincture from all this. Throughout the
period the traditional image of the frail ship venturing into the
power of the unpredictable and uncontrollable sea must have
become more alive for writers, even if they never went to sea,
surrounded by stories of expeditions, and knowing how great
was the investment in these voyages, in terms of money,
reputation, status, and power, and how much depended on a
successful outcome. Although it would be impossible to
measure and describe the full impact of maritime activity on

1

literary metaphor, it is one of the aims of this book to consider
ways in which there may be positive links between real and
metaphoric voyages.

To explore these links is not, however, my primary aim. My
work in recent years on the narratives of actual voyages from
the sixteenth to the eighteenth century made me more sensitive
to the presence of voyage as metaphor in imaginative writing. I
use 'metaphor' in a wide sense, whenever a journey by ship
means more than itself. It can be an isolated figure of speech,
as in Othello's remark (which provides the title of this book)
when, after the murder of Desdemona, he says:

> Heere is my journies end, heere is my butt
> And verie Sea-marke of my utmost Saile.

I mean also the elaborate similes in *Paradise Lost*, the
allegorical voyages in *The Faerie Queene*, Donne's extension
of actual voyages into emblem and symbol, as in his verse
letters, 'The Storme' and 'The Calme', fables such as *New
Atlantis*, or the image of the writer as voyager, as used by both
Spenser and Bacon.

For quite a number of Renaissance writers, I thought, the
voyage metaphor was not of fundamental importance: for Ben
Jonson and George Herbert, for example, although I shall
later be using isolated metaphors from both of them. (In
Jonson's *Catiline* there is some quite extensive voyage
imagery but it does not have significance for the play as a
whole.) But for my six chosen writers, voyage imagery seemed
an indispensable element in the construction of individual
works, and, to some extent, though not perhaps for Shakespeare and Milton, an element of fundamental importance for
understanding their work as a whole. Although there are
arresting differences among the six in the ways in which the
metaphorical element manifests itself, and in the kind of effect
it has, I kept finding that to approach a quite familiar work
through its voyage imagery was to gain a new insight and
understanding.

The initial and abiding purpose of this book is explicatory; to explain how the metaphor of the voyage is built into different works by different writers and why it is essential to the elucidation of the work in question. In the three chapters which form the Shakespeare section, for example, I first argue that if the implications of that single image of the sea-mark are examined and pursued through *Othello*, a view of the play and the hero emerges which is wholly opposed to the prevailing evaluation of the last half-century. In the *Macbeth* chapter, though I offer no such general re-interpretation, I suggest that some scattered allusions to voyaging, especially in two of the witches' scenes, inject a subliminal voyage motif into the play which adds considerable depth of perspective and shading. In the third chapter I look at reasons for Shakespeare's strange determination to force shipwrecks into the stories he chose for his comedies and romances. Each of these chapters is an independent and autonomous essay in interpretation; and this is the case not only for the Shakespeare section but for the book as a whole. What unites the separate essays—apart from showing how flexible, volatile and powerful the metaphor of the voyage was in this period—is the contribution which each has to offer to two related subjects or themes.

The leading theme will be obvious enough. A sea-mark is something that guides a seaman to his objective, and I give emphasis to the word because it is the definition of a voyage that it has a motivation, an end in view. A ship was a useless thing, Donne said more than once, unless it were at sea with a purpose (see pp. 78 and 80). Drifting is the negation of voyaging; here again Donne provides a text, with the terrifying picture of frustration in 'The Calme', and there is another text in Rosse's image for the helplessness of the people of Scotland under Macbeth (pp. 126–27). A voyage is a journey somewhere, and the crucial word in this book is navigation. Navigation has to do with the control of one's life, with the direction in which one is heading, or believes one is heading. 'The Master in the Shippe is judged by the directing his course

aright, not by the fortune of the Voyage', wrote Bacon
(p. 158). Navigation has to do with the extent of one's
personal power to reach a destination, good or bad, and the
extent of supernatural power, good or bad (including of
course Fortune) to help or hamper one's efforts. The issue of
'navigation' is at the centre of *Macbeth*. The deep-seated
acceptance by the hero of his freedom to shape his own life is
countered by his certainty that it is otherwise. 'Thou marshall'st me the way that I was going', he says to the air-borne
dagger (p. 123). The issue is also central to *Othello*, whose
hero looks back on his life as a course plotted by false
navigational aids. Issues about the control of one's life, about
responsibility for deflection and disaster, are at the heart of
Elizabethan tragedy, and of all serious writing besides. Those
who wrote the narratives of the real voyages of the time were
equally preoccupied by these problems as they reflected on the
misadventures that had befallen them, as I have shown in other
writings.[1]

The issue of control and destination is fought out in the
voyage imagery of Spenser's *Faerie Queene*, in which there is a
prolonged battle for dominance—as though they were two of
his own allegorical knights—between wandering and purposeful self-direction. There is no battle in Bacon's writing, but the
effort he exerted to make the navigation of uncharted waters
the central image for both intellectual and moral life, culminat-
ing in the essay 'Of Adversitie', is one of the main subjects of
my Bacon chapter. But whoever takes up the metaphor of the
voyage becomes involved in the question of control and the
destination of life, and there is a different perspective in every
chapter. Debate is not always obvious; it has not (to my
knowledge) been perceived as the central issue of Donne's
'Hymne to God my God, in my sicknesse'.

One way in which this debate conducts itself is in a radical
questioning whether a voyage is or is not an appropriate image

1 See Edwards (1992) and (1996).

for the course of human life. Such questioning is tacit in *The Faerie Queene* but is explicit in Donne (see p. 79). The image of the voyage, though it may suggest human frailty and feebleness, also suggests determination to achieve a future, to shape one's own ends, to defy obstacles; it may therefore be incongruent with an ideal of life as submission, patience, and meditation. The image is correct for Bacon, and for him the patron saint of voyages is Hercules, sailing in a pitcher to relieve the sufferings of Prometheus. The image is false for Milton, for whom the patron saint of voyages is Satan himself, winging his way to occupy and destroy God's new created world. In Marlowe's plays, the questioning takes the form of a complex oscillation of sympathy, for and against two kinds of self, the passive Dido and the aggressive Tamburlaine.

The debate about the control of life, as it becomes a questioning whether the voyage is a fit image of the lives we live or should live, is (in the hundred years time-span of this book) a continuation of an age-old debate on the morality of travel. I introduce this theme in the Milton chapter, and describe it and its ramifications more fully in the Conclusion. Here I say no more than that the argument against travel bases itself on a primeval time of happiness when travel was simply unnecessary. All travel, it follows, is a mark of the loss of that happiness, a mark of discontent, and a restless search for what has been lost.

This double concept of voyaging as on the one hand the restless search of the discontented, and on the other as determined self-creation, is a formidable presence in the writings I discuss, and it is at this point that I wish to go back to the relationship between the new vitality in the voyage imagery of sixteenth- and seventeenth-century writers and the real voyaging of that time.

Writers in the past, such as Walter Raleigh in his essay, 'The English Voyages of the Sixteenth Century', for the 1903–05 reprint of Hakluyt's *Principall Navigations*, or, in America, R. R. Cawley in *Unpathed Waters: Studies in the Influence of the Voyagers on Elizabethan Literature* (1940), tended to stress how the enthusiasm and excitement felt by English writers for the courage and enterprise of their compatriots on behalf of the nation were reflected in their work. Enthusiasm is there, certainly, but it exists in a perpetual conflict with other reactions which temper and qualify it. The objectives of voyaging were wealth, power, and the subjugation of others; and these objectives were questioned as much as they were accepted. I came to see the tension or friction between enthusiasm and disapproval as the main source of the new energy in voyage metaphors. The voyage of a sailing ship at sea is almost by definition a two-faced Janus of a metaphor; being on the one hand an image of successful struggle and on the other an image of human helplessness in the face of greater powers. This equivocation was immensely sharpened in the period I am concerned with by perplexity about the ethics of contemporary ventures. A stock image about storm or tides or rocks or steering or cargo or havens could become a receptacle of conflicting implications. Instead of elucidating or enforcing a statement, the metaphor might introduce hesitation and qualification. Uncertainty about the motivation and character of voyaging tended to create uncertainty wherever the literary image of the voyage appeared. This is especially true of Marlowe and Donne, and (in a very different way) it is true of Milton. It is even true of Bacon, although his hesitation and uncertainty are minimal.

The first part of this book is devoted to the three writers, Spenser, Marlowe and Donne, in whose metaphoric voyages I find most strongly these contrary movements. The last part sets Bacon against Milton, enthusiasm against disapproval, though I show how both enthusiasm and disapproval are qualified. Where in this does Shakespeare stand? This debate about the ethics of contemporary voyaging affects his work less than anyone else's. Even though he used the 'Bermuda pamphlets' of 1609 in composing *The Tempest*, though Maria in *Twelfth Night* talks about 'the new Mappe, with the augmentation of the Indies', though the ship, the *Tiger*, in the vengeful plans of the First Witch in *Macbeth* has been identified with a real ship that went to Aleppo, though trading voyages are the necessary environment of *The Merchant of Venice*, it is not by the route of his voyage metaphors that Shakespeare engages with contemporary issues of building a nation and an empire. Even in *The Tempest*, the play most deeply concerned with imperial and colonial problems, the voyages themselves belong with the fantasy of Antigonus' voyage to the sea-coast of Bohemia in *The Winter's Tale*. And that includes Gonzalo's hymn to the role of Providence in directing events.

The innocence of Shakespeare's voyage metaphors towards the activities of Frobisher, Hawkins and Drake, and the aspirations of Ralegh and Hakluyt, may seem disappointing, but it is not my wish to build bridges which will not bear traffic. In my book, *Threshold of Nation*, published in 1979, I dealt as fully as I could with the engagement of Shakespeare's plays with the issues of nation and empire, including the relevance of *The Tempest* to questions of colonization. This is another book: through the lens of his voyage metaphors Shakespeare cannot be seen taking part in a debate which the same lens shows other writers to be deeply concerned with. There is nothing in that area touching on the morality of England's efforts to extend her trade and possessions by sea.

*   *   *   *   *

In the songs and sonnets of the late sixteenth and early seventeenth centuries there are innumerable voyage images and conceits, and for the most part they do not rise above conventional and expected applications. I have selected three short poems, by Fulke Greville, Thomas Wyatt and Samuel Daniel, in which I find the use of the voyage metaphor of unusual interest, and I am going to examine these partly to represent the use of the voyage metaphor outside my six chosen writers, and partly to illustrate how even these short

works can contribute to the issues about navigation and the
ethics of the voyage which thread this book.

> Who ever sailes neere to *Bermuda* coast,
> Goes hard aboord the Monarchy of Feare,
> Where all desires (but Lifes desire) are lost,
> For wealth and fame put off their glories there.
>
> Yet this Ile poyson-like, by mischiefe knowne,
> Weanes not desire from her sweet nurse, the Sea;
> But unseene showes us where our hopes be sowne,
> With woefull signes declaring joyfull way.
> *For who will seeke the wealth of Westerne Sunne,*
> *Oft by* Bermuda's *miseries must runne.*
>
> Who seeks the God of *Love*, in Beauties skye,
> Must passe the Empire of confused Passion,
> Where our desires to all but Horrors die,
> Before that joy and peace can take their fashion.
>
> Yet this faire Heaven that yeelds this Soule-despaire,
> Weanes not the heart from his sweet God, *Affection*;
> But rather shewes us what sweet joyes are there,
> Where constancy is servant to perfection.
> Who *Caelica's* chast heart then seeks to move,
> Must joy to suffer all the woes of *Love*.[2]

The dating of Greville's poetry is very uncertain; this probably
belongs to the end of the sixteenth century. By that time the
dangers to shipping off Bermuda had been described in many
narratives. The traditional conceit comparing the progress of
love to a voyage is given more than topicality and immediacy
by the invocation of real voyages. In the process of making the
comparison, the 'vehicle' (real voyages) comes under scrutiny
even as it strives to illuminate the 'tenor' (the search for

2 Fulke Greville, *Caelica*, Sonnet LIX. Text from *Poems and Dramas*,
ed. Geoffrey Bullough, 1939, i, 109.

heavenly beauty). The passage off the coast of Bermuda, traditionally hostile to sailors, is seen as an intense purgatorial experience, in which fear strips away the unworthy desires for wealth and fame which dominated the venturer. The transformed sailor is not deterred, and continues—in some manner—his voyage. The miseries of Bermuda are the necessary prelude to fulfilling what one most hopes for, which is 'the wealth of Westerne Sunne'. By a strange alchemy the voyage and the sought-for gold have been transmuted into some more spiritual endeavour and reward. Or else the search for real gold has in some way become sanctified by suffering.

Then comes the application. 'Who seeks the God of *Love* in Beauties skye . . .' The monarchy of fear off the Bermuda coast becomes for the platonist lover the empire of confused passion, an experience of horror which strips away false desires and strengthens true desire, encouraging the lover in the pursuit of his affection for Caelica's chaste heart. If we take it that Caelica is a real woman, love for whom is to be regarded as the first stage of a love of heavenly beauty, we assume the meaning of the second stanza to be that the resumed search for real gold is legitimate if the heart be right. If we follow the more likely assumption that Caelica *is* heavenly beauty, then the sailor in the second stanza has abandoned his voyage, and, a sadder and a wiser man, is seeking some more spiritual benefit.

The awkwardness of the poem lies in the difficulty of dematerializing the objective of the voyage. The cleansing that is attempted in 'the wealth of Westerne Sunne' looks like a mere verbal asylum. Greville realizes what Donne (as will be seen) only part of the time realizes, that when voyaging and spiritual life are brought into comparison the material rewards of voyaging may contaminate the religious aspirations; but in trying to prevent the contamination he has led the poem into confusion.

Fifty or sixty years before Greville wrote his poem, and before most of the voyages which Hakluyt collected had even been thought of, Sir Thomas Wyatt wrote a fine poem in which he, like so many other writers before and after, used the capricious sea to express his doubts about responsibility for the course of his life. I take this poem as a kind of negative evidence: to show that the force of voyage imagery does not depend on topicality and the impact of the real. The poet, in his role as rejected suitor, imagines himself at sea, and addresses Venus (Cytherea). No mention here of Bermuda coast.

Though this thy port and I thy servaunt true,
And thou thy self doist cast thy bemes from hye
From thy chieff howse, promising to renew
Boeth joye and eke delite, behold yet how that I
Bannysshed from my blisse carefully do crye:
'Helpe now Citherea, my lady dere,
My ferefull trust *en vogant la galère.*'

Alas the dowbt that dredfull absence geveth;
Withoute thyn ayde assuraunce is there none;
The ferme faith that in the water fleteth
Succour thou therefor; in thee it is alone.
Stay that with faith that faithfully doeth mone,
And thou also gevest me boeth hope and fere,
Remembre thou me *en vogant la galère.*

By sees and hilles elonged from thy sight,
Thy wonted grace reducing to my mynde,
In sted of slepe thus I occupy the nyght;
A thowsand thoughtes and many dowbtes I fynde,
And still I trust thou canst not be unkind,
Or els dispere my comfort, and my chiere
Would fle fourthwith *en vogant la galère.*

Yet on my faith full litle doeth remain
Of any hope whereby I may my self uphold,
For syns that onely wordes do me retain,
I may well thinck the affection is but cold;

But syns my will is nothing as I would,
But in thy handes it resteth hole and clere,
Forget me not *en vogant la galère*.[3]

This is a poem about 'fereful trust'. The doubtful poet is as much asking Venus to confirm that she *can* help him, as he is beseeching her to reward his dedication to her. His 'ferme faith' in her power 'fleteth' in the water—floats uncertainly. And he depends entirely on her to achieve the scarcely defined objective of his lady's love. His own will, he says, 'is nothing as I would'. But his plea to the goddess to confirm his weakening faith in her power is undercut by the refrain which ends each stanza, *en vogant la galère*. There was, and is, a proverbial saying, *Et vogue la galère*; let the boat sail where it will, come what may, befall what may befall. It is an expression both of resignation and acceptance, acknowledging the total control of Fortune. The poet is asking Venus to guide his boat if she possibly can, but his language suggests it's a lost cause, because the boat is controlled by Fortune. In his great poem, 'My galy charged with forgetfulnes', based on Petrarch and also using the image of a voyage, Wyatt wrote, 'The starres be hid that led me to this pain'. This significantly enlarges the reference of Petrarch's line: *'Celansi i duo miei dolci usati segni'* , the two accustomed sweet signs—presumably the beloved's eyes—hide themselves.[4] By calling the eyes stars, Wyatt transcends the immediate object of desire, and speaks about that which directs the course of his life. The feeling that the betrayal he is speaking of in 'the starres be hid that led me to this pain' relates to spiritual desertion and ultimate loss is greatly strengthened by the poem to Venus we are now discussing, in which flagging faith looks for a sign it does not expect to receive. In both poems Wyatt uses the metaphor of the voyage for a condensed and highly charged

3 Text based on *Collected Poems*, ed. Muir and Thomson, Liverpool, 1969, p. 59.
4 *Ibid*, pp. 289–90.

representation of doubt and distress about the control and
direction of his life.

Samuel Daniel's poem, 'Ulisses and the Syren', was published in 1605. It is a version of the debate between love and
duty which can be found in Sidney's *Astrophil and Stella*,
Marlowe's *Tamburlaine*, or Donne's 'Canonization'.

> *Syren.* Come worthy Greeke, *Ulisses* come
> Possesse these shores with me;
> The windes and Seas are troublesome,
> And heere we may be free.
>   Here may we sit, and view their toile
> That travaile in the deepe,
> And joy the day in mirth the while,
> And spend the night in sleepe.
>
> *Ulis.* Faire Nimph, if fame, or honor were
> To be attaynd with ease
> Then would I come, and rest me there,
> And leave such toyles as these.
>   But here it dwels, and here must I
> With danger seeke it forth,
> To spend the time luxuriously
> Becomes not men of worth.
>
> *Syr. Ulisses,* O be not deceiv'd
> With that unreall name:
> This honour is a thing conceiv'd,
> And rests on others fame.
>   Begotten onely to molest
> Our peace, and to beguile
> (The best thing of our life) our rest,
> And give us up to toile.
>
> *Ulis.* Delicious Nimph, suppose there were
> Nor honour, nor report,
> Yet manlines would scorne to weare
> The time in idle sport.

For toyle doth give a better touch,
To make us feele our joy;
And ease findes tediousnesse as much
As labour yeelds annoy.

Syr. Then pleasure likewise seemes the shore,
Whereto tends all your toyle,
Which you forgo to make it more,
And perish oft the while.
  Who may disporte them diversly,
Finde never tedious day,
And ease may have varietie,
As well as action may.

Ulis. But natures of the noblest frame
These toyles, and dangers please,
And they take comfort in the same,
As much as you in ease.
  And with the thought of actions past
Are recreated still;
When pleasure leaves a touch at last,
To shew that it was ill.

Syr. That doth opinion onely cause,
That's out of custome bred,
Which makes us many other lawes
Then ever Nature did.
  No widdowes waile for our delights,
Our sportes are without bloud,
The world we see by warlike wights
Receives more hurt than good.

Ulis. But yet the state of things require
These motions of unrest,
And these great Spirits of high desire,
Seeme borne to turne them best,
  To purge the mischiefes that increase,
And all good order mar:

For oft we see a wicked peace
To be well chang'd for war.

   Syr. Well, well *Ulisses* then I see,
I shall not have thee heere,
And therefore I will come to thee,
And take my fortunes there.
   I must be wonne that cannot win,
Yet lost were I not wonne:
For beauty hath created bin,
T'undoo, or be undonne.[5]

This intelligent and subtle poem gives a much better balance between the contestants than Spenser provides between Phaedria and Guyon (see pp. 19–20). The archetype of voyagers does not insist that fame and honour are sufficient motives for a life of action. Sheer 'manliness' demands it, and it is not only a satisfaction in itself, but it increases the sense of pleasure—when there's time for it. One's feeling of identity depends on achievement ('With the thought of actions past / Are recreated still'). In the last stanza but two, the Siren simply rejects Ulysses' argument that the urge for action is innate. Ulysses, she says, is talking about the laws of custom, not of nature. Ulysses therefore shifts his ground from nature to historical circumstances. 'The state of things require / These motions of unrest.' It is ambitious men who must mould the times to what he calls 'good order'. The ending is remarkable. The Siren will have to go with Ulysses. If she can't win, she has to be won—has to be defeated. As I understand the poem, Daniel means that the state of rest and the state of unrest cannot coexist; there must be either the one or the other. If unrest prevails, it portends the destruction of beauty.

So here voyaging is the emblem of restless energy, of the need to keep moving and to change things, of the need to

5 Text from *Poems and A Defence of Ryme*, ed. A. C. Sprague, Harvard University Press, 1930, pp. 161–63.

create a self by tangible achievement. No doubt whatsoever that this poem takes part in the pro- and anti-travel debate. Behind the seductiveness of the Siren and her proffer of a life of love and mirth there is a very serious invitation to abandon a life of effort which is against nature. It is interesting how often the voyage to the riches of east or west is used as a symbol of contemporary unrest. In an anonymous poem in William Byrd's *Psalmes, Sonets & Songs* of 1588 in praise of the pastoral life there is the following stanza.

> All day their flocks each tendeth,
>   At night they take their rest;
> More quiet than who sendeth
>   His ship into the East,
> Where gold and pearle are plentie,
>   But getting, very daintie.[6]

It is only by paying attention to the metaphor of the voyage in each of these three poems that one can come at its meaning. And in each the metaphor extends the poem into a forum where the direction of life and the direction of lives are debated. What is true of these poems is true also of the larger bodies of writing which I now go on to examine.

6 There is a modernized text in Norman Ault's *Elizabethan Lyrics*, under the title 'The Quiet Life'.

PART ONE

CHAPTER ONE—SPENSER
'Who fares on sea,
may not commaund his way'

Faire Sir (quoth she) be not displeasd at all;
Who fares on sea, may not commaund his way,
Ne wind and weather at his pleasure call:
The sea is wide, and easie for to stray;
The wind unstable, and doth never stay.
But here a while ye may in safety rest,
Till season serve new passage to assay;
Better safe port, then be in seas distrest.
Therewith she laught, and did her earnest end in jest.
(II.vi.23)[1]

These words are spoken by Phaedria to Guyon in Book II of
Edmund Spenser's *The Faerie Queene*. Phaedria is a lady full
of merriment and song who runs a crooked ferry-service on
the Idle Lake. She takes those passengers she chooses to her
island, a place of paradisal loveliness, and tempts them to yield
to a life of pleasure. She has already waylaid Cymochles, who
was bound on a mission of revenge, and now she has taken up
Guyon, who is on his quest to destroy the Bower of Bliss. She
has refused to allow both men the company of their watchful
attendants, Atin and the Palmer.

With these platitudes about the dangers and uncertainties of
sea-travel Phaedria tries to calm Guyon's anger at being led
astray . Her advice falls midway between the literal and the
figurative. Guyon is for the moment a sea-traveller; though
it's an inland sea, it's big enough to lose sight of land (xi.4;

---

1 Quotations from *The Faerie Queene* are from J. C. Smith's edition
(Oxford: Clarendon Press, 1909, reprinted 1972), with the letters u, v, j
normalized.

xii.2). But Phaedria is at the same time making a comment on life, using sea imagery in a general proverbial way. It is no wonder that at the end she punctures her own solemnity with a laugh. She is no doubt amused as much by the banality of her wise saws as by their inappropriateness. They are certainly inappropriate on the literal level. Phaedria has a remarkable boat, a 'litle Gondelay', which is not in the least subject to wind and weather; not only is it a fast power boat, which she controls by turning a pin, but it has automatic navigation.

> Ne cared she her course for to apply:
> For it was taught the way, which she would have,
> And both from rocks and flats it selfe could wisely save.
> (II.vi.5)

Phaedria is not subject to the elements; she is one of the few people in the poem who knows exactly where she is going and how to get there, and she has reached her destination. She has got Guyon where she wants him, and neither he nor she has drifted to this haven.

She fails, however, in her intent. Guyon will have nothing to do with her. He resists her blandishments and persuasions and subdues his sexual desire (vi.26, 6). The hedonism of accepting a life of pleasure that unexpectedly offers itself is repugnant to a young man determined to reach his goal. Phaedria accepts her failure. So, in spite of her gondelay, she comes in the end within the circuit of the maxim that had so amused her: 'Who fares on sea, may not commaund his way'.

When Guyon gets ashore, Spenser sends him on his way with a voyage simile suggesting all the confidence in navigation which Phaedria's maxim and her experience deny.

> As Pilot well expert in perilous wave,
>   That to a stedfast starre his course hath bent,
>   When foggy mistes, or cloudy tempests have
>   The faithfull light of that faire lampe yblent,
>   And cover'd heaven with hideous dreriment,

Upon his card and compas firmes his eye,
The maisters of his long experiment,
And to them does the steddy helme apply,
Bidding his winged vessell fairely forward fly:

So *Guyon* having lost his trusty guide,
    Late left beyond that *Ydle lake*, proceedes
    Yet on his way, of none accompanide;
    And evermore himselfe with comfort feedes,
    Of his owne vertues, and prayse-worthy deedes.

                                        (II.vii.1–2)

Guyon has refused to accept the philosophy of the safe port, and here the poet backs him up by denying the proposition that who fares on sea may not command his way. Though he has for the moment lost his guide, Guyon has the moral training and fitness to steer his way through the hazards of life to his destination. The self-reliance of the Christian voyager could hardly be more strongly indicated.

Such voyaging images as we get in the Phaedria/Guyon episode are of first importance in *The Faerie Queene*, describing the progress of the poet himself as well as the progress of his characters.[2] They are very common; they mostly tell of storms and dangers of the sea, delaying or diverting or destroying the mariner as he strives to keep on his course and reach his desired port; but sometimes they speak of happy arrival after stress and difficulty, or respite in an unexpected haven. Their common concern is the effort to reach a destination or objective in adverse circumstances. They often seem sententious and platitudinous, but we should beware of copying Phaedria in mocking their triteness.[3]

2 See the excellent entry by Jerome S. Dees in *The Spenser Encyclopedia* (ed. Hamilton), s.v. ship imagery, and his earlier article, 'The Ship Conceit in *The Faerie Queene*', 1975.
3 Dees has much to say (in 'The Ship Conceit') on the significance of what is ostensibly commonplace or a cliché.

Voyage images relating to the poetic venture are interestingly placed at the end of the first and the end of the last book of *The Faerie Queene*. Canto xii of Book I opens with a resounding nautical image heralding the end of the story of Una.

> Behold I see the haven nigh at hand,
>   To which I meane my wearie course to bend;
>   Vere the maine shete, and beare up with the land,
>   The which afore is fairely to be kend,
>   And seemeth safe from stormes, that may offend;
>   There this faire virgin wearie of her way
>   Must landed be, now at her journeyes end:
>   There eke my feeble barke a while may stay,
> Till merry wind and weather call her thence away.

In the final stanza of the Book, Spenser tells 'ye jolly Mariners' to strike their sails:

> For we be come unto a quiet rode,
> Where we must land some of our passengers.

When the ship is repaired and restocked she will 'againe abroad / On the long voyage whereto she is bent'.

> Well may she speede and fairely finish her intent.

Canto xii of Book VI, published six years later, opens with the rather defiant assertion that in spite of every detour and delay, he is still on course.

> Like as a ship, that through the Ocean wyde
>   Directs her course unto one certaine cost,
>   Is met of many a counter winde and tyde,
>   With which her winged speed is let and crost,
>   And she her selfe in stormie surges tost;
>   Yet making many a borde, and many a bay,
>   Still winneth way, ne hath her compasse lost:

> Right so it fares with me in this long way,
> Whose course is often stayd, yet never is astray.

Then, for describing the career of characters, the main voyage images relate to Guyon in Book II (already noted), Britomart and Arthur in Book III, and Calidore in Book VI.

Britomart first. Seeking Artegall, whose image she has fallen in love with, she has reached Faeryland, and 'searching all lands and each remotest part, / Following the guidance of her blinded guest'—that is, Cupid—she has come to the seashore, where she watches the surge beating against the rocks, and she makes her complaint, three stanzas long. She is a feeble vessel, tossed about on a huge sea of sorrow, in danger of shipwreck and death. Love is her pilot and fortune is her boatswain, but they are of no help; they 'saile withouten starres gainst wind and tide'. So she prays to Neptune, promising to honour him if he brings her safely to her destination.

> Thou God of winds, that raignest in the seas,
>> That raignest also in the Continent,
>> At last blow up some gentle gale of ease,
>> The which may bring my ship, ere it be rent,
>> Unto the gladsome port of her intent:
>> Then when I shall my selfe in safety see,
>> A table for eternall moniment
>> Of thy great grace, and my great jeopardee,
> Great *Neptune*, I avow to hallow unto thee.
>
> (III.iv.10)

Almost immediately she survives the great encounter with the wrathful Marinell, who tries to forbid her passage over the Rich Strond; he falls beneath her spear, like an animal brought to the sacrifice (stanza 27). In time, she and Artegall meet quite by accident (IV.iv.39; vi.9).

The image attaching to Prince Arthur is very brief. His wanderings in search of Gloriana have been interrupted by his hot pursuit of the fleeing Florimell. Night falls and he loses sight of her.

> Like as a ship, whose Lodestarre suddenly
> Covered with cloudes, her Pilot hath dismayd;
> His wearisome pursuit perforce he stayd,
> And from his loftie steed dismounting low,
> Did let him forage.

He lies down, but sleep eludes him because his mind is running on Florimell.

> Oft did he wish, that Lady faire mote bee
> His Faery Queene, for whom he did complaine:
> Or that his Faery Queene were such, as shee.
>
> (III.iv.53–54)

In Book VI, Calidore, in his exhausting pursuit of the Blatant Beast, comes across the shepherds. The attractiveness of their simple and tranquil life is a good deal enhanced for him by the attractiveness of Pastorella, and he speaks to Meliboe.

> Give leave awhyle, good father, in this shore
> To rest my barcke, which hath bene beaten late
> With stormes of fortune and tempestuous fate,
> In seas of troubles and of toylesome paine,
> That whether quite from them for to retrate
> I shall resolve, or backe to turne againe,
> I may here with your selfe some small repose obtaine.
>
> (VI.ix.31)

This is a restatement, in another key, of Phaedria's view of things: 'Here a while ye may in safety rest' . . . 'Better safe port, then be in seas distrest'. We have come a long way from the image of Guyon's determined, skilful (and successful) navigation of his life. Britomart felt herself helpless among the waves and prayed (successfully) to the god of the seas. The brief image relating to Arthur interestingly subverts faith in navigation because the lodestar itself, the magnet of his existence, is no longer steady. Florimel begins to take the place of his Faerie Queene.

All these images of the sea-voyage are superimposed on the basic journey images that form the substance of *The Faerie Queene*, its 'continued Allegory, or darke conceit'. And sometimes of course these journeys are by water, so that in interpreting the metaphor we are working on two rather than three levels. So, in the last canto of the second book, Guyon is making a real voyage on the inland sea (which had formerly done duty as the Idle Lake) towards the Bower of Bliss.[4] Guyon is no longer, as he was in the 'superimposed' image at the beginning of Canto vii, the skilled navigator of a sailing vessel. He is being rowed by a brawny Boatman, and steered by the Palmer—a crew in strong contrast with the Boatswain (Fortune) and the Pilot (Love) of Britomart's conceit. The Boatman tells the Palmer to 'stere aright, / And keepe an even course'. They successfully negotiate the terrors of the Gulfe of Greedinesse and the Rocke of Vile Reproach, resist the renewed allurements of Phaedria, avoid the Quicksand of Unthriftyhed and the Whirlepoole of Decay, circumvent monsters of the deep and siren mermaids, before reaching land. We are watching Guyon's successful completion (with help from outside) of a traditional maritime obstacle course, easy to interpret.

Guyon's voyage is just one part of the vast complex of journeys that make up the allegoric narrative of *The Faerie Queene*. But although it is perhaps the most clearly defined journey in *The Faerie Queene*, with a setting out, a route maintained, and an arrival at a destination, it is, of course, wholly removed from voyaging in the real world, and it shares the perverse dream-like inconsequence of all travel in Spenser's poem. As Graham Hough wrote: 'A castle or a cave

4 For analogues and the significance of Guyon's voyage, see Nellist (1963).

or a lake appears when it is required by the narrative situation; but we never feel it has been arrived at by a geographical journey'.[5] To understand the changing role of the image of the voyage in *The Faerie Queene*, we need to set the voyage within the context of travel in general within the poem.

Finding the proper route, keeping to it and progressing along it—all of which dominate the allegory of Bunyan's *Pilgrim's Progress*—play a very small part in Spenser's allegorical procedures, even in the first two books, each of which is dominated by the quest of the hero. In the early stages of Book I, sticking to the proper path, or wandering from it, is allegorically important for the Red Cross Knight (e.g., I.i.28, I.ii.12), but the imagery is not maintained, and, considering the absence of milestones, it is a surprise to be told at the beginning of Canto xi that we have 'now approched neare' to Una's wasted kingdom, and are on her 'native soyle'. The concordance gives over half the sixteen references in *The Faerie Queene* to 'path' or 'paths' to this first book, but a number of these relate not to the Red Cross Knight's route towards the dragon, but to the 'litle path, that was both steepe and long', leading to the New Jerusalem, which is pointed out to the Knight by the hermit as the route he must follow when he has done his worldly tasks.

Only very rarely in *The Faerie Queene* do readers feel that they are accompanying the characters along a route in any particular direction. Knights have objectives and missions, but there are no highways to be kept, no sense of getting nearer. A reader feels he or she is moving round a great Italian church, taking in one magnificent fresco after another. It is almost as though the characters do not themselves travel, but are visited by the allegorical experiences they are to encounter. So, Guyon and the Palmer, having 'measurd many miles', spy at sunset 'a goodly castle, plast / Foreby a river in a pleasaunt dale', and we enter the set scene of the House of Temperance.

5 Hough, p. 96.

The rich arbitrariness of faerieland travel is nowhere better demonstrated than in the first canto of Book III. Arthur and Guyon are travelling together on what would seem to be a very long journey: 'Full many Countries they did overronne', meeting unspecified dangers and perils, and achieving 'many hard adventures'. They come across a knight and in the usual ferocious encounter are discomfited; the knight turns out to be Britomart. They travel on together, going nowhere in particular.

> Long they thus travelled in friendly wise,
>   Through countries waste, and eke well edifyde,
>   Seeking adventures hard, to exercise
>   Their puissance, whylome full dernely tryde:
>   At length they came into a forrest wyde,
>   Whose hideous horror and sad trembling sound
>   Full griesly seem'd: Therein they long did ryde,
>   Yet tract of living creatures none they found,
> Save Beares, Lions, and Buls, which romed them around.
>   (III.i.14)

Then out of the thickest brush gallops a goodly lady on a milk-white palfrey, pursued by a lustful forester. It is Florimell, whose errand is here left unexplained. Guyon and Arthur go after Florimell, but Britomart 'forward went, / As lay her journey, through that perlous Pace'. She gets out of the wood, spies a stately castle, and her adventure in Castle Joyeous begins. No map, Elizabethan or modern, could conceivably convey these wanderings, which range far and wide and yet remain within a confine so limited that every traveller can meet every other. With Britomart, the impression is given of purposeful travel, but she is in fact wandering without any fixed route or known destination.

Wandering is a fundamental feature of romance. Its importance in *The Faerie Queene* was considered by Angus Fletcher in *The Prophetic Moment* (1971). His argument was that the motive power of the poem was the interaction of two great archetypes, the temple and the labyrinth. Temples are places of order and fulfilment; labyrinths of unmapped disorder, of terror and panic[6]—and are characterized in particular by wandering. The labyrinth is Faerieland as a whole; temples are within the labyrinth, containing, straightening out, harmonizing the disorder of the labyrinth. Following Mircea Eliade, Fletcher viewed wandering in the labyrinth as a rite of passage leading toward the trial and initiation of the hero. Each of the two archetypes has its parodic opposite: the temple can appear as a prison, and wandering can be both a search for structure and sheer error.[7]

The Prophetic Moment was an Apollonian book, believing that Spenser had got it right, was on top of things, and in the end 'proves an ultimate cosmic constancy'.[8] To place the problem of wandering within the tectonic collision of archetypes was a masterly strategy, but in the end it demands extreme faith in the tightness and consistency of the Spenserian *Weltanschauung*. The proposed scheme does not really fit the particularities of individual journeying in the poem. To concentrate on these journeys, by sea and by land, all of them metaphoric at their different levels, is to become aware of very marked changes in the value given to journeying as an image of purposeful moral life, changes which are strongly marked in the voyage images, and which are prepared for by an indifference from the start to the importance of route-keeping.

It is noticeable that directionless travel increases greatly in Books III and IV, and it does not really lessen in Books V and VI, in which the idea of the heroic quest resumes, with the missions of Artegall and Calidore. The purpose of travel tends to become less of an attempt to reach a place than a search for a missing person, or an escape, or a pursuit. All of these involve wandering rather than progress along a route. The words of

6 Fletcher, pp. 29, 13.
7 *Ibid.*, 35–36, 43.
8 *Ibid.*, p. 218.

Calidore, explaining his quest to Artegall at the beginning of Book VI, are especially significant.

> But where ye ended have, now I begin
>   To tread an endlesse trace, withouten guyde,
>   Or good direction, how to enter in,
>   Or how to issue forth in waies untryde,
>   In perils strange, in labours long and wide,
>   In which although good Fortune me befall,
>   Yet shall it not by none be testifyde.
> What is that quest (quoth then Sir *Artegalll*)
> That you into such perils presently doth call?
>
> The Blattant Beast (quoth he) I doe pursew,
>   And through the world incessantly doe chase,
>   Till I him overtake, or else subdew:
>   Yet know I not or how, or in what place
>   To find him out, yet still I forward trace.
>   (VI.i.6–7)

In the later books of *The Faerie Queene*, as the intercrossing and uncompleted narratives multiply, the sense of travel is much diminished, and we feel that we are in a theatre, with every new character begetting a new story to be told, taking us further and further away from the possibility of concluding any one of them. The reader's perplexity in keeping track of the stories seems matched by Spenser's breathlessness as he claims that he can hardly keep abreast of the increasing intricacy of his narrative. Book VI is full of what look like naive asides in which the poet tells us he will have to leave x for a moment while he tells us about y. Isabel MacCaffrey notes how often in Book VI the ordered containment of the canto-structure is violated with 'self-conscious wielding of the narrative shears'.[9]

Books IV–VI were published in 1596, three years before

9 MacCaffrey (1976), p. 336*n*.

Spenser died (at the age of about 47). No more of the poem is
known to exist, except for the great Mutability Cantos, which
concluded the poem when it was reprinted in 1609, ten years
after the poet's death.

For a long time now, Spenser criticism has been almost as
much concerned with the collapse or failure of Spenser's grand
design, as with the elucidation of that design. The explanatory
letter to Ralegh, printed at the end of the first three books in
1590, was not repeated in the six-book *Faerie Queene* of 1596.
It spoke of the groundwork of the poem as a twelve-day feast
kept by the Faery Queene, on each day of which a knight,
representing one of the twelve moral virtues, was to set out on
his adventures. The purpose of the entire 'continued Allegory'
was 'to fashion a gentleman or noble person in vertuous and
gentle discipline'. The great endeavour to contain the vehem-
ence and ferment of mortal life within the fragile vessel of a
poem begins confidently with the completed quests of Red
Cross to subdue the satanic dragon and of Guyon to destroy
Acrasia's Bower of Bliss. In 1590 the poem ended with the
rapturous union of Scudamour and the rescued Amoret at the
end of Book III. But when the first three books were
republished with a further three in 1596, that closure at the end
of Book II was unsealed; Scudamour and Amoret were kept
apart, not to re-unite within the lifetime of the poem. Within
the growing tangle of intercrossing stories in Books IV–VI
there are some completions: Artegall slays Grantorto, and
Calidore gives the Blatant Beast a drubbing, though it escapes.
Marinell and Florimell are united. But these successes do not
have the triumphalism of the successes of Red Cross and
Guyon, and they are in the shadow of the uncompleted
stories—particularly those of Britomart, Amoret and Scudamour, and Prince Arthur. Almost more important is the
change from concentration on a single major hero in the first
two books to the crowded scenes of the later books, in which
we may lose sight of the hero and his quest for long periods.
The ways through Faerieland have indeed become, as Spenser

describes them at the beginning of the proem to his last book, 'exceeding spacious and wyde'.

The question, a very familiar question, is whether we have been denied by Spenser's comparatively early death the completion of his epic vision of human life, or whether in 1596 the poem came to a stop, because it had nowhere to go. Nowhere to go except for that brilliant posthumous conclusion of the Mutability Cantos, which in a way rephrase the question—whether in a universe of perpetual change and instability the idea of order is sustainable.

In her 1976 book, *Spenser's Allegory: The Anatomy of Imagination*, Isabel MacCaffrey used Spenser's own ship imagery to enforce her view that the incompleteness of *The Faerie Queene* reflects Spenser's awareness of the limitations of art. 'The poet who steers his course through the poem does not reach a haven, and not merely because he was prevented from finishing his work.' 'The great poem ends with a repudiation of fictions and a confession of the human limits of imagining.' 'Only God can write the ultimately satisfying poem, and it will not be an allegorical fiction.'[10] Later, *The Faerie Queene* was a major concern of Balachandra Rajan in his 1985 book, *The Form of the Unfinished: English Poetics from Spenser to Pound*. Rajan drew a distinction between 'incomplete' and 'unfinished' poems. 'Unfinished poems are poems which ask not to be finished, which carry within themselves the reasons for arresting or effacing themselves as they do.' Spenser is left with 'the problem of bringing about the sense of an ending within the accumulating likelihood of a stalemate.' Can 'the fictive enclosure . . . be relied on to safeguard its contents?' Rajan suggests that 'the poem's interrogation of itself . . . almost seems to presage challenges to come in literary history of the Apollonian principle by the Dionysiac'[11].

10 *Ibid.*, (1976), pp. 400, 431, 432.
11 Rajan, pp. 14, 9, 56, 75.

What does Spenser's voyage-imagery add to the debate about closure in *The Faerie Queene*? Jerome Dees was surely right in his contention that the use of voyage-images both for the poet himself and for his heroes demonstrated, by the end of the unfinished poem, a growing scepticism 'about the power of heroic action to embody the highest ideals of virtue' and a lessening of the narrator's confidence in his poetic structure. 'The ship conceit ... operates structurally to remind us of the similarities between heroic endeavours to achieve temperance, or chastity, or justice and the equally heroic act of writing a poem whose aim is to instruct a nation.'[12]

Faith in the idea of an individual life as the determined overcoming of obstacles in the progress towards a spiritual or moral trophy became exhausted not so much during as through the writing of *The Faerie Queene*: 'Whatever flames upon the night / Man's own resinous heart has fed.'[13] The poem came to a halt in 1596 because further advance was not profitable or possible. The confidence at the end of Book I that the ship-poem could tackle its long voyage and land its passengers at the intended ports could not be maintained. The voyage image has succumbed to the strength of the sea; the sea has proved stronger than the vessel which sails on it. 'The yesty Waves / Confound and swallow Navigation up.'[14] This is not Spenser's defeat. Quite the reverse. It is his victory to acknowledge the fallibility of his (and everyone else's) 'feeble barke'.

The success of a navigator depends absolutely on his ability to master or collaborate with the power of the sea. The decline of the voyage image has to be seen in the context of the symbolism of the sea, especially in Books III and IV.[15] The

12 Hamilton, *Encyclopedia*, s.v. ship-imagery, and Dees, p. 212.

13 W. B. Yeats, 'Two Songs from a Play'.

14 See p. 117.

15 Kathleen Williams has much that is helpful on the symbolism of the sea; e.g. *The World of Glass*, pp. 139–45, and her 1970–71 article, 'Spenser:

much pursued Florimell, chased by a monster that feeds on women's flesh, gets to the sea-shore and plans to drown herself. But she finds a boat, leaps in and pushes it out to sea (III.vii.27). The boat drifts with the tide (viii.21), and when the sleeping fisherman wakes, Florimel asks him 'to guide the cock-bote well'. This makes the lecherous fisherman 'fondly grin'; he answered that 'his boat the way could wisely tell'. The fisherman has his own meaning for 'cockboat'; the actual boat continues to drift as he assaults her—Spenser makes a point of it. When Proteus in answer to her screams drives his sea-chariot to the rescue, he finds the 'wandring bote, / That went at will, withouten carde or sayle' (viii.31). There is an obvious contrast with Phaedria's boat, which guided itself to whatever destination its owner chose, and also with Guyon's boat, moved through difficult conditions by the combined efforts of the Palmer and the Boatman. Florimell is wholly at the mercy of the sea, whose protection she has sought. Assaulted by the fisherman, she is rescued by Proteus and taken to his bower at the bottom of the sea. And then the sea-god presses his attentions on her, taking on every shape to win her love; when she refuses him he imprisons her in a deep dungeon. And there Florimell remains for seven months, chained and in darkness, surrounded by the roaring sea and ten thousand monsters (IV.xi.i–iv).

Florimell is desired by every male being, mortal, faery, or god, who sees her, except the one she loves, Marinell (a Faerie knight with a mortal father and a goddess mother).[16] Mari-

Some Uses of the Sea and the Storm-tossed Ship'. Thomas Roche's book, *The Kindly Flame*, remains of great importance for Books III and IV.

16 Where she saw him to fall in love with him, Spenser does not say. Her early history is very shadowy. Her dwarf Dony tells Arthur in III.v that she left court on hearing that Marinell had been worsted in fight, and that she had sworn not to return until she found him, dead or alive. But when she was first seen, fleeing on her palfrey, Britomart was present, and Britomart had not yet encountered Marinell. Her objectives and motives have been supplied to her retrospectively, while she is already on the move.

nell's mother is the daughter of the god Nereus, the Old Man of the Sea. (She is called Cymoent in Book III, but this is changed to Cymodoce, after Virgil, in Book IV.) The most interesting aspect of Marinell is his wealth. At Cymodoce's request Nereus made Marinell the richest man in the world by bestowing on him all the riches of the sea, all that sunken treasure which so kindled the imagination of Elizabethan writers and which Spenser describes in two wonderful stanzas (III.iv.22–23). So Marinell is enriched 'through the over-throw / And wreckes of many wretches', and these wretches continue to bewail their loss which is his store. The other notable thing about Marinell is his fear of woman's love, instilled in him by his mother, who mistakenly interpreted the prophecy of Proteus that her son would be undone by 'a virgin strange and stout'. But it is the armed strength of a woman, not a woman's love, that shatters him. The sacrificial felling of Marinell by Britomart (III.iv.17) is a major event which takes place immediately after Britomart's prayer to Neptune. Her defeat of the redoubtable champion of the sea's worth casts a shadow over the symbolic value of the union of Marinell and Florimell. The beauty of the earth is married to an enfeebled scion of the sea, and the union is poetically enfeebled (V.iii.1–3).

Marinell eventually goes to Proteus' subaqueous home to attend the Thames-Medway wedding, and hears the lament of the imprisoned Florimell. 'Know *Marinell*', she cries, 'that all this is for thee' (IV.xii.5–11). Marinell is deeply struck. Back home in his mother's bower he pines with desire for his admirer. When his mother learns that this is love-sickness she sues to Neptune himself to make Proteus release Florimel, 'a waift, the which by fortune came / Upon your seas'. Neptune issues the order, and Proteus reluctantly gives up his captive. Then in two-and-a-half stanzas, concluding Book IV, it is all over. Cymodoce admires Florimell's beauty, takes her home to Marinell, who was 'revived with her sweet inspection'. Florimell is given no reaction to her release or her meeting with her long-sought beloved except for the remarkably subdued final lines of the book.

> Ne lesse was she in secret hart affected,
> But that she masked it with modestie,
> For feare she should of lightnesse be detected:
> Which to another place I leave to be perfected.

We hear at V.ii.4 that they are to be married 'at the Castle of the strond'. The first three stanzas of Canto iii speak of Florimell's joy in terms of the sun showing his face 'after long stormes and tempests'.

> So when as fortune all her spight hath showne,
> Some blisfull houres at last must needes appeare.

She is made the 'joyous bride' of Marinell at a wedding that 'infinite great store' of lords and ladies attend, but Spenser dismisses the solemnities with a brief gesture—'worke fit for an Herauld, not for me'—and gets on with the tournament, and the arrival and extinction of the false Florimell.

The union of Florimell and Marinell has been emptied of meaning. Florimell's devotion is in the first place puzzlingly opportunistic on Spenser's part, and whatever it was meant to signify has become etiolated during the writing of Book IV. As a victim of the sea, she is surely one of the richest examples of the sea's treasure, which is built up by the overthrow and wreck of humankind (III.iv.22). Since this treasure was heaped on Marinell by Nereus there is a fitness in Marinell acquiring her as a bride. But to be acquired seems too passive a role for Florimell. Some positive accommodation between beauty and the power of the sea must have been intended by her marriage to Marinell; some amelioration of the sea's rage; some giving back to mankind of that great store of treasure wrested from it by misfortune.[17] Whatever was intended has

---

17 See further in my essay, 'The Rapture of the Sea', in *Shakespearian Continuities*, ed. J. Batchelor, T. Cain and C. Lamont, 1997.

not been achieved; the immense poetic preparation runs into the sands. The union of Florimell and Marinell can do nothing to abate or reduce the overwhelming power of the sea. The strength of Florimel as a symbol lies in her weakness. Strong and determined as a person, she pursued a shadow and was pursued by reality. She remains a drifting victim of the sea: its imprisoned treasure.

The union which really matters in Book IV is that of the Thames and the Medway, which Spenser most certainly did not consider 'worke fit for an Herauld, not for me'. Their wedding is the real success story which drives that of Florimell and Marinell off the front page. Rivers have perfect commerce with each other and with the sea. They join each other and fulfil themselves by being absorbed into the ocean—even Irish rivers.

> All which long sundred, doe at last accord
>   To joyne in one, ere to the sea they come,
> So flowing all from one, all one at last become.
>   (IV.xi.43)

'The natural movement of the river from source to mouth reflects an idealized cycle of life in which there are proper and healthy relationships . . . between male and female,' writes James Broaddus. But he goes on to say, 'Florimell and Marinell will be able to share the kind of love that comes so naturally and effortlessly to the Medway and the Thames.'[18] Possibly this was within Spenser's plan, but it is not in his performance. The rivers, and in particular the Thames and 'the Bride, the lovely *Medua*', are not personifications of humanity; they are rather a kind of reproach to men and women whose happy unions and successful missions are becoming increasingly difficult to chronicle.

All the sea-gods attend the wedding, a confusion of gods, who, though they process in tranquil agreed order, might be

18 Broaddus, pp. 50 and 58.

thought to be in contention for 'the powre to rule the billowes, and the waves to tame': great Neptune and his queen, and the many sons who were founders of puissant nations; aged Ocean and his dame Tethys; Nereus their eldest son; and most impressively the fifty daughters of Nereus, the Nereides, 'all goodly damzels, deckt with long greene haire'; Spenser gives the names of all fifty of them (IV.xi.48–51). The sea is in their immediate charge; they bring about or end its storms, and they rescue survivors from wrecks (xi.52). Every member of this pantheon has power to control the waves. To put it the other way round, this great assembly is the assembly of the names which humanity has given to the superhuman powers imagined to control the uncontrollable sea. And the sea is an emblem of life itself.

Canto xii opens with a hymn to 'the seas abundant progeny', a lyrical celebration of fecundity which is an obvious reference back to the Garden of Adonis (III.vi), providing a parallel or complementary source of generation and fertility.

> For much more eath to tell the starres on hy,
> Albe they endlesse seeme in estimation,
> Then to recount the Seas posterity:
> So fertile be the flouds in generation,
> So huge their numbers, and so numberlesse their nation.
>
> (IV.xii.1)

And sure enough, Venus appears in the next stanza, '*Venus* of the fomy sea was bred'. It is her spirit that endlessly augments the richness of the world's multiplicity.

However it came about that the 'Two Cantos of *Mutabilitie*', with two further stanzas, were added to the posthumous republication of the six-book *Faerie Queene*, they seal the unfinished work with a finality so absolute and satisfying that you cannot think the author was not in some mysterious and hidden manner engaged in providing them. In another and more authoritative way, the cantos rework the basic idea of

Books III and IV that the unpredictable changefulness of the
sea cannot be mastered or overruled.[19]

The subject of the two cantos is the challenge of the titaness
Mutability to be recognized and accepted as the dominating
power in the world, as against the establishment gods, Jove in
particular, who obtained their power by conquest. The claim
is that the true order of the world is disorder: continuous
change, impermanence, instability. Mutability's case is
referred to Nature, greater than any god, who changes from
male to female in the second canto. Her famous judgement
(vii.58) is that change is indeed the rule of life, but that change
is a sort of refinement and fulfilment of the being that is
changed. Therefore, that which is changed maintains its state.
This sophistry has a venerable history,[20] but it remains a
contradiction in terms unless we agree that the word change
applies only to outward appearance and integument. More
important than this scholasticism is her vision of a future when
Time shall be no more and there will be no more change. The
Canto ends very abruptly.

> So was the *Titaness* put downe and whist,
> And *Jove* confirm'd in his imperiall see.
> Then was that whole assembly quite dismist,
> And *Natur's* selfe did vanish, whither no man wist.

That Jove is confirmed in his imperial see until the end of
time may be a statement of fact; it is hardly the moral
judgement that comes from the poetry. 'Mutability is oddly
convincing', wrote Kathleen Williams.[21] Why 'oddly' I do not
know, but she is certainly convincing. She is a being of
surpassing beauty, a beauty 'that could the greatest wrath
soone turn to grace', and even Jove is affected by it (vi.28, 31).

19 For a résumé of the continuing debate about the Cantos, with
documentation, see Parker, pp. 54–7, 250.

20 See Fletcher, pp. 226–27.

21 Williams (1966), p. 228.

The chief evidence of the primacy of change which she produces before Nature is the procession of the seasons and the months (vii.28–46), a procession of the greatest beauty. No case is made out on the other side; the Olympian right is the right of possession. Mutability's challenge is that Jove and his crew are impostors. Not only do they have no right to rule—they do not in fact rule. They only pretend they are the causes of what happens (vii.49)—like witch doctors who claim to cause eclipses of the sun. Neptune's claim to rule the sea is a sham (vii.27). What is unanswerable in Mutability's case is that Jove is 'begotten . . . And borne here in this world' (vii.53). As Kathleen Williams wrote, Mutability's argument is that the Olympian gods are 'mythological figures, dependent for their existence upon the wavering thoughts of men'.[22] The gods are 'mortall borne' and their names, natures and functions are constantly changing. If we go back to those sea gods, we see that they too are only human dreams, grasping at communications which may influence the future. The power of Neptune, like the power of Jove, is not in any sense real.

At the end of the Mutability Cantos, Nature confirms that Jove is in charge. But that does not mean any more than saying that humanity will always invent metaphysical forces to try to explain the vicissitudes of life, and to express their longings and hopes. In the two stanzas of 'Canto vii', the poet turns right away from the Apollonian factory to—to what? To an expression of longing and hope for the stability of eternity. 'O that great Sabbaoth God, graunt me that Sabaoths sight.'

The defence of Apollonian systems in the Mutability Cantos is slight in substance and in argumentative weight. Such systems are manufactured by human beings for their social needs and personal desires. What comes across most powerfully in these cantos is an acceptance of the world as *varium et mutabile*, a recognition that change and fluctuation have their own beauty:

22 *Ibid.*, p. 230.

> The birds that range
> From cloud to tumbling cloud,
> Minute by minute they change.[23]

Perhaps the most potent of all the gods in *The Faerie Queene* is Proteus, the sea-god whose shape is always changing, who knows the future but whose prophecies are misunderstood. He is capable of rescuing and preserving what is most beautiful and desirable, and also of imprisoning it in 'eternall thraldome'. His surrender of Florimell to Cymodoce on the orders of Neptune has the same factitious quality as the subordination of Mutability to Jove.

Ordered poems delineating ordered lives require an ordered cosmos. It is an acceptance that instability and the unpredictable are more certain presences than order and meaningfulness that frays the clear pattern of missions as *The Faerie Queene* progresses, and leaves the poem uncompleted and uncompletable.

In this connection, the story of Bracidas and Amidas in Book V, Canto iv, is very important. They are brothers, and each was left an island of the same size. But the 'devouring Sea, that naught doth spare', eroded the elder brother's island and threw up the land on the island belonging to Amidas. In time a chest full of treasure, which Amidas claimed, was washed up on the island belonging to Bracidas. To Amidas Artegall says that the land which the sea plucked away from his brother and brought to his island is rightfully his own. 'What the sea unto you sent, your owne should seeme.' And to Bracidas he says that since the sea has sent him the chest, that is rightfully his. 'What the sea unto you sent, your owne should seeme.'

> For what the mighty Sea hath once possest,
> And plucked quite from all possessors hand,
> Whether by rage of waves, that never rest,
> Or else by wracke, that wretches hath distrest,

23 W. B. Yeats, 'Easter 1916'.

He may dispose by his imperiall might,
As thing at randon left, to whom he list.

(V.iv.19)

Territory and wealth, given and taken away, haphazardly
and unpredictably. Fortune and misfortune, irrationally and
unforeseeably offered, to be accepted with gratitude or fortitude. The sea gives, and the sea takes away.

The final voyage-image of importance in *The Faerie Queene*
relating to one of the characters was that used by Calidore
when he finds the pastoral peace of the shepherds.

Since then in each mans self (said *Calidore*)
    It is, to fashion his owne lyfes estate,
    Give leave awhyle, good father, in this shore
    To rest my barcke, which hath bene beaten late
    With stormes of fortune and tempestuous fate,
    In seas of troubles and of toylesome paine,
    That whether quite from them for to retrate
    I shall resolve, or backe to turne againe,
I may here with your selfe some small repose obtaine.

(VI.ix.31)

At the beginning of Canto x, the narrator is stern with
Calidore, that, 'entrapt of love, which him betrayd', he has
become 'unmyndfull of his vow and high beheast' laid on him
by the Faery Queene, but reflects that he is not greatly to be
blamed. Indeed not, for he is given the vision of Mount
Acidale, with the hundred maidens dancing about the three
Graces, and in the midst Colin Clout piping to his love. And
his own love, Pastorella, turns out to be the scion of a noble
family. He does indeed renew the search for the Blatant Beast,
finds it and belabours it. But his achievement is of no account,
as the bitter ending of Book VI makes clear, with its description of malice and slander growing worse in the world, and
venomously attacking Spenser's own poem.

The idea of gratefully accepting a haven when blown off

course was presented by Phaedria to Guyon. She dismissed it with her own laughter, for she with her clever boat thought herself immune from mishaps. Guyon rejected it because it falsified his own conception of life as a self-directed struggle. In Book VI, the axiom has much more force. 'Who fares on sea, may not commaund his way.'

The last person to be convinced of the direction his poem is going in seems to be the poet himself, who, as we saw, opens the last canto of Book VI with his assurance to the reader that his ship-poem is still on course towards 'one certaine cost'. The compass has not been lost; all detours and delays are more apparent than real; the course 'is often stayd, yet never is astray'. There are other interpretations of this stanza, besides that which sees Spenser still doggedly pursuing the scheme outlined in the letter to Ralegh. The stanza could be ironic; Spenser might be assuming the guise of Phaedria, mocking his own asseverations. Or perhaps the ship, like so many Elizabethan ships, is making for another harbour than the one originally intended. Lines 6 and 7 of this stanza seem very important.

> Yet making many a borde, and many a bay,
> Still winneth way, ne hath her compasse lost.

This is not to say that *in spite of* being driven to many coasts and bays the ship is still on her original course, but that it is progressing *by means of* coming to these places. Everywhere the poem goes is where the poem is going. In fact, as a voyage of heroic effort and achievement, it will shortly come to an end. Perhaps the true north of the compass has become 'that Sabaoth sight', figuratively to be presented in Calidore's vision of Mount Acidale.

The sea is greater than the vessel which sails in it. The image of careful and skilful navigation has become inappropriate as an image of human endeavour, and at that point the image becomes inappropriate for the poet too. *The Faerie Queene* is an attempt to contain or tame the violence of the sea; to win back the treasure it has stored up from the wreck of human lives. In time, the poem is also a recognition that only rivers can live in constant harmony with the sea.

* * * * *

It is obvious what a study of voyage metaphor in *The Faerie Queene* has to contribute to the issue of 'navigation' or the control of one's life. It remains to ask what it has to contribute to the second issue, namely, the association of the metaphor with contemporary voyaging. Or, to put it another way, to ask how far the navigation issue is political. What does the metaphor signify in the context of the voyaging that was going on all the time that Spenser, himself a voyager between England and Ireland, was writing *The Faerie Queene*? We should begin with the perspective of genre.

Patricia Parker has described the nature of romance as a series of detours and suspensions which are always postponing the achievement of quests and the realization of objectives.[24] In a sense, therefore, the contest in *The Faerie Queene* between episodic wandering and purposeful journeying can be seen as the genre quarrelling with itself. In Book VI Spenser yields to the conventional contours of romance. Parker stresses the significance of the last completed book being a pastoral; Spenser and his hero Calidore have relaxed into the repose of the historical origins of romance.[25]

The political implications of the opposition of romance and its wanderings to purposeful voyaging were studied in an important essay by David Quint published in 1985, 'The Boat of Romance and Renaissance Epic'.[26] Quint made a distinction between the wandering boat of Fortune, taking the hero from adventure to adventure, characteristic of the

24 Parker, especially pp. 4 and 220.
25 *Ibid.*, pp. 107–13.
26 See References. The essay was later incorporated in the book *Epic and Empire: Politics and Generic Form from Virgil to Milton*, Princeton, 1993, as Chapter 6, 'Tasso, Milton, and the Boat of Romance'.

romance, and the purposeful voyage of a hero carrying out a quest, characteristic of the epic. He illustrated the difference by contrasting the wanderings in an enchanted boat in Tasso's early romance *Rinaldo* with the purposeful voyage of Fortune's boat in *Gierusalemme liberata*, 'an essential part of the epic machinery that drives forward to the providential goal and narrative endpoint of Tasso's poem'. In keeping with its aristocratic mien, the epic in adopting the voyage had to translate its commercial aims into heroic aspiration. The archetype here is Camões' celebration of Vasco da Gama in *Os lusíadas*.[27] In Quint's terms, then, one might say that Spenser strove to inject the purposefulness of epic into romance, and failed. How may we translate this generic fluctuation into political terms?

The Faerie Queene has always been recognized and read as a political poem; in its adulation of Queen Elizabeth, its fervent endorsement of the national religion, in its celebration of the national past, and its veiled running commentary on personalities and events. The difference in the approach of the 'new historicism' of recent years has been its determination to relate every feature and every aspect of the poem to its socio-political matrix. Stephen Greenblatt's chapter on Spenser in *Renaissance Self-fashioning* spoke of him as 'our originating and preeminent poet of empire' and argued that his great medievalizing poem was throughout informed by the issues of nascent imperialism, in particular 'the European response to the native cultures of the New World' and 'the English colonial struggle in Ireland'.[28] The centre of his argument was that the description of the Bower of Bliss and its destruction by Guyon mirrors or rather symbolically manifests the encounter of the colonizer with the colonized.

27 Quint argues that in *Paradise Lost* Milton mocks this translation by putting the voyages in a specifically commercial setting and relating them to Satan's journey, which itself is demoted from epic by being made subject to Fortune.
28 Greenblatt, pp. 174, 179.

Greenblatt's theory of the psyche of imperialism was that the aggressive impulse was a dangerous compound of desire and suppression. Freud's notion that civilization depended upon renunciation or at least 'the controlled satisfaction of instinct' is used to characterize the attraction and repulsion experienced in the encounter with the inhabitants of newly discovered lands. Guyon's voyage to the Bower of Bliss represents actual voyages of discovery, and his destruction of its heady voluptuousness represents 'our culture's violent resistance to a sensuous release for which it nevertheless yearns with a new intensity'.[29] The whole of *The Faerie Queene* bespeaks this 'intense craving for release, which is overmastered only by a still more intense fear of release'. The questing knights are, as it were, in a state of perpetual disappointment as they pursue 'the principle of regenerative violence'.[30]

There is not much help here with generic fluctuation: the compound psyche operates with consistent force. But clearly the diagram of the mind as a site of combat between two opposed impulses allows for one side or another to dominate on occasion. At one point, Greenblatt associates the suppression of desire with 'disillusionment'.

> Each heroic quest is at once a triumph and a flight, an escape from the disillusionment glimpsed for a brief moment on the Mount of Contemplation and again at the close of the Mutabilitie Cantos.[31]

This perception is taken no further, but to hint at a scepticism which 'would undermine the rightness of the moral mission'[32] opens the way to unevenness of allegiance in the texture of the poem.

29 *Ibid.*, p. 175.
30 *Ibid.*, p. 188.
31 *Ibid.*, pp. 178–79.
32 *Ibid.*, p. 179.

Writing fourteen years later than Greenblatt, Gary Waller, in his book *Edmund Spenser: A Literary Life* (1994), which is sympathetic to the New Historicist approach, concentrates on the 'dislocation' between the spirit and manner of the first three books of *The Faerie Queene* and that of the last three. In part (he suggests) the dislocation represents the tensions and stress operating on the Protestant poet in Elizabethan England. 'Spenser, as *The Faerie Queene* becomes seemingly more and more beyond his capacities to finish or control, rejects his own poetic creation as an example of the mistrustful promiscuity of worldly signification.'[33] More specifically, he suggests that during his visit to England after writing the first three books Spenser became disillusioned with what he found.

> *The Faerie Queene*, the most ambitious glorification of the Elizabethan regime, could no longer unambiguously celebrate the power which permitted it to exist without revealing the strains and contradictions that were already radically dislocating that power.[34]

Greenblatt and Waller, for both of whom *The Faerie Queene* is inalienably the child and product of its time, differ in their description and explanation, but agree on the coexistence of antithetical forces in Spenser's engagement with the national enterprise, whose emblem was Gloriana and whose agents were ships on the high seas. Waller is clear that the continuance of the poem and Spenser's faith in the national enterprise are interdependent.

It is worth comparing the vocabulary of the later twentieth century for describing Spenser's divided mind with that of the beginning of the century. In his essay on Spenser written in 1902, W. B. Yeats expressed his conviction that Spenser's commitment to English Protestant nationalism and imperialism was a denial and a betrayal of his essential poetic self. Here

33 Waller, p. 23.
34 *Ibid.*, 139.

was 'a system of life which it was his duty to support'—though it reads more like brain-washing than duty. His 'thoughts and emotions . . . had been organised by the state.' 'The image of the State . . . had taken possession of his conscience'; he 'learned to look to the State . . . as the maker of right and wrong.' Throughout Elizabethan literature, however, Yeats felt that there was 'a quarrel to the death with that new Anglo-Saxon nation', and that Spenser, 'the first poet who gave his heart to the State, was also 'the first poet struck with remorse'.[35] The remorse, it is implied, lies not in Spenser's 'conscious art', but in those parts of his poetry which Yeats felt to be comparatively free from the official morality, and which he included in the selection of Spenser's verse to which his essay was an introduction.

The two strands in Spenser's poetry as Yeats distinguishes them are not quite differences of genre but it is a strongly political distinction that he is making. However we look at it, the wavering in the use of the metaphor of the voyage, the distance between Guyon the determined pilot and Calidore resting in harbour, is a wavering in Spenser's commitment to Gloriana. There is no question of a conscious variation in commitment. The harsh and uncompromising *View of the Present State of Ireland* is a late work, and that the man who wrote it was the poet who wrote the later books of *The Faerie Queene* is painfully apparent in Book V, with the unrelenting and unquestioning ferocity of its conception of justice.

In spite of the attractiveness of Greenblatt's identification of Guyon's voyage with real voyages of discovery, the level of correspondence between actual and metaphorical voyaging is very distant. When in Book VI, Canto xi, 9, the slave-traders descend on the island where the brigands hold Meliboe and his people captive, the writing strongly suggests the activities of Sir John Hawkins off the African coast. But this note of realism only emphasizes the innocence of the metaphoric and

35 Yeats, pp. 365, 369, 371, 372, 373.

symbolic voyages of *The Faerie Queene*. They know nothing of the actualities of Hawkins or any other Elizabethan adventurer, and there is no level of reading on which they can bring these actualities to mind. Spenser differs sharply in this from Donne, and Marlowe, and Milton. What they do reflect, however, is the spirit of purposefulness which generated the entire imperial enterprise.

The voyage image is anterior to the political commitments which it includes and embraces. The variation in its employment, persuasively represented as a clash of the competing genres of epic and romance, suggests not so much a change of heart but the presence from the beginning of cross-currents and opposed allegiances, and the gradual domination of the unofficial and unrecognized allegiances. The defeat of the image of purposeful voyaging, I have suggested, has been foreshadowed from the beginning of the poem. Its precariousness casts a shadow of doubt and uncertainty over the whole of Spenser's commitment.

I conclude by turning to Yeats again, to a strange poem which he called 'Gratitude to the Unknown Instructors'. It is connected with *A Vision*, and presumably relates to what he had learned from the occult communications transmitted to his wife. I imagine it was intended that the second sentence should be seen as the consequence of the first sentence. But, as it stands, the poem voices a gigantic disjunction between two ideas totally opposed to each other, the second cancelling out and denying the first.

> What they undertook to do
> They brought to pass;
> All things hang like a drop of dew
> Upon a blade of grass.

An ideal of life as purposeful endeavour and successful achievement is balanced against the conception in Marvell's poem, 'On a Drop of Dew', in which the true life of the spirit is independent of the transitory material existence to which it is slenderly and uncertainly attached. The two perceptions lie side by side without explanation. The first two lines may represent Spenser beginning his great poem and Guyon setting out from Phaedria's island. The second two represent Calidore at rest with the shepherds, and the Mutability cantos which round off an unfinished epic. Whether Spenser himself was ever consciously 'disillusioned' is questionable, but the poetic force of the Mutability cantos strongly persuades us that the authority of Neptune and Jove, and of all others who undertake to shape the future, is illusory.

CHAPTER TWO—MARLOWE
'Ransacke the Ocean
for orient pearle'

And here not far from *Alexandria*,
Whereas the Terren and the Red Sea meet,
Being distant lesse than ful a hundred leagues,
I meant to cut a channell to them both,
That men might quickly saile to *India*.
        Tamburlaine, Part 2; 5. 3. 131–35.[1]

Christopher Marlowe's work, full of the excitement of open-ing up new worlds of knowledge and riches, makes very little use of the traditional tropes of the sea. The following is exceptional:

No more dismaide with tidings of his fall
Than in the haven when the Pilot stands
And viewes a strangers ship rent in the winds,
And shivered against a craggie rocke.
        Tamburlaine, Part 1; 4. 3. 31–34.

So is the following—a part of Leander's seductive rhetorical patter:

A stately builded ship, well rig'd and tall,
The Ocean maketh more majesticall:
Why vowest thou then to live in *Sestos* here,
Who on Loves seas more glorious wouldst appeare?
        Hero and Leander, 1, 225—28.

---

1 Quotations from Marlowe, except for *Dr Faustus*, are from the Oxford edition by C. F. Tucker Brooke, 1910, with some minor editing, and with act, scene and line references normally from the editions in the Revels series. Quotations from *Dr Faustus* are from the parallel texts edition by W. W. Greg, Oxford, 1950.

The characteristic Marlovian note is not in simile or metaphor
like these but in evocation. Here Callapine, son of Bajazeth, is
trying to persuade his keeper to release him.

> A thousand Gallies mann'd with Christian slaves
> I freely give thee, which shall cut the straights,
> And bring Armados from the coasts of Spaine,
> Fraughted with golde of rich *America*.
> > *Tamburlaine*, Part 2; 1. 2. 32–35

In these contexts the voyage is the image of desire; with the
vision of the riches of newly discovered worlds often linked
with the search of Jason for the Golden Fleece. There is,
however, a counter-image in Marlowe, in which the voyage is
an image of separation.

In three plays of Marlowe the sea plays a vital role. The
locality is sea-girt; arrival and departure are by ship. This is
obviously the case with the island-play, *The Jew of Malta*, and
also with *Dido, Queen of Carthage*, which wholly depends on
the arrival and departure of Aeneas by sea. But it is also the
case with the much more land-locked *Edward II*, which apart
from one French scene is firmly located on English soil. Its
England is an island, surrounded by the sea, with hostility on
the far side of it—except on the Scottish border, where
hostility has no barrier. Curiously, in the famous passage (Act
2, scene 2) in which the barons taunt Edward with the victories
of Scotland, Marlowe keeps the sea-surround in mind by
making Mortimer interpose with the gibe that 'the hautie
Dane commands the narrow seas, / While in the harbor ride
thy ships unrigd'.

England is the kingdom, the homeland, divided against
itself by the anger of the nobles against the king's infatuation
with Gaveston. Gaveston comes from over the sea, from
France. He would have swum, like Leander, if necessary (1. 1.
8–9). His arrival completes Edward's happiness, but destabil-
izes the body politic. The separation which the proud barons

try to enforce will literally be Gaveston's renewed exile across the sea, but this deportation becomes heavily symbolic.

> . . . Sooner shall the sea orewhelme my land,
> Then beare the ship that shall transport thee hence.
> 1. 1. 151–52

Or, with the king identifying himself with his land:

> Ere my sweete *Gaveston* shall part from me,
> This Ile shall fleete upon the Ocean,
> And wander to the unfrequented Inde.
> 1. 4. 48–50

Gaveston sails to Ireland. The nobles hope and Edward fears he will be shipwrecked; again literally and figuratively. There is much play on this crossing of the sea: the nobles see him as a 'torpedo'—a dangerous fish—floating dead on the Irish Sea (1. 4. 224). His return to England is marked by one of the many references in the play to favourable and unfavourable winds helping or hindering ships.

> The winde is good, I wonder why he stayes,
> I feare me he is wrackt upon the sea.
> 2. 2. 1–2.

Edward sends the queen and their son to France: 'Madam, we will that you with speed be shipt . . .' (3. 2. 81). After Gaveston has been killed, France becomes the place of disaffection, where plotting against the king is nourished. 'Faire blowes the winde for Fraunce', cries Edmund, duke of Kent, 'blowe gentle gale, / Till *Edmund* be arrivde for Englands good' (4. 1. 1–2).

Eventually the winds , 'prosperous windes', blow the queen and her allies back to England. The king, hard pressed in the fighting that follows, is persuaded by his new favourite, Spencer, to flee to Ireland. This attempt to divide himself from his kingdom fails; they take ship, but 'awkward windes and sore tempests' (4. 6. 34) drive them back on shore, and

Edward has to face the long-drawn-out sacrilegious rites of his suffering and murder, the fulfilment, as it were, of Lancaster's gruesome image at the start of the play of the throne as a boat drifting on a sea of blood (1. 1. 130–31). Two final images of oversea exile strikingly suggest the re-establishment of a stabilized homeland under the new king Edward III. Matrevis, who assisted at Edward's murder, reports back to Mortimer. Fearing betrayal, he pleads 'let me flie'. Mortimer's curt reply is, 'Flie to the Savages'. And when he, Mortimer, is condemned to death by the new young king, he goes out with this:

> Farewell faire Queene, weepe not for *Mortimer*,
> That scornes the world, and as a traveller,
> Goes to discover countries yet unknowne.
> 5. 6. 64–66

The sea is an important presence in *Edward II*, islanding the troubled homeland and differentiating it from the 'elsewhere' to the influence of which it is nevertheless so vulnerable. But the sea is never in the forefront of the play as it is in the earlier *Dido, Queen of Carthage*.

In view of Marlowe's contemptuous treatment of ideas about divine intervention in human affairs in *Tamburlaine* and *The Jew of Malta*,[2] it is surprising that in *Dido* he should have taken over from Virgil the wholesale domination of human affairs by the gods. Aeneas' fleet is belaboured and scattered by the storm raised by Juno, but he is brought to safety by Jupiter. Dido falls in love with Aeneas because of Cupid's work on behalf of Venus; their love is consummated by reason of the storm raised by both Venus and Juno; Aeneas leaves Carthage because of the visitation of Jupiter's ambassador Hermes/Mercury. Yet the sardonic introduction of Jupiter as pederast idling his time away with Ganymede makes fun of the theodicy which Marlowe has taken over. Jupiter's role as

2 See Edwards (1990), pp. 128–31.

omnipotent ruler of the universe is further undercut by
Marlowe's alteration of Virgil's account of the calming of the
storm. In the Aeneid, the watchful Jupiter notices that
something is wrong and angrily intervenes; in *Dido* it is Venus
who is angry—with Jupiter, that he can 'sit toying there . . .
with that female wanton boy' while Aeneas is in peril on the
wild sea. Jupiter's prophecy of the future decreed for Aeneas
and the Trojans is received by Venus with some impatience:
while Jupiter is talking Aeneas continues to be in danger. 'I
will take order for that presently [i.e., at once]', Jupiter replies
meekly. Marlowe is not taking Roman ideas about divine
control very seriously.

The adversity which Aeneas is battling with on the high seas
is more than Juno's spite. He is an exiled wanderer, and the
malevolent ocean has its traditional role of adversity in general
(1. 1. 52–53, 223). The very interesting imagery given to
Venus compares the hostility of the waves to the attacks of the
Greeks.

> Poore *Troy* must now be sackt upon the Sea,
> And *Neptunes* waves be envious men of warre,
> *Epeus* Horse, to *Ætnas* hill transformd,
> Prepared stands to wracke their woodden walles,
> And *Æolus* like *Agamemnon* sounds
> The surges, his fierce souldiers, to the spoyle.
>
> 1. 1. 64–69

In this image, the adversity of the sea becomes the adversity of
the Trojan war, and the adversity of the Trojan war becomes
the adversity of the sea.

King Iarbas, would-be lover of Dido, sees Aeneas as an
alien visitor, 'a Phrigian far fet o' the sea' (3. 3. 64).[3] He wants
to see him 'shipt away, / And hoyst aloft on *Neptunes* hideous
hills'. The wanderer has come to a temporary haven; how

3 I accept Brooke's emendation for the original 'to the sea'; unfortuna-
tely the Revels editor chooses 'forfeit to the sea'.

permanent will it be? Marlowe inserts into Virgil's story a first
abortive attempt by Aeneas to leave Dido. 'Nobilitie abhors to
stay'; 'I may not dure this female drudgerie' (4. 3. 19, 55).
Dido's blandishments quickly change his mind. In a remarkable passage, he dedicates himself to Dido in images of voyage.

> O *Dido*, patronesse of all our lives,
> When I leave thee, death be my punishment.
> Swell raging seas, frowne wayward destinies,
> Blow windes, threaten ye Rockes and sandie shelfes,
> This is the harbour that *Æneas* seekes,
> Lets see what tempests can anoy me now.
>
> 4. 4. 55–60

'O blessed tempests that did drive him in!', exclaims Dido.
But she knows the pressure on him to leave and seek Italy. Her
longing to keep him takes strange forms. She wishes she had
the winds and the sea in her control, to convert the voyage into
a passage of love:

> That he might suffer shipwracke on my breast,
> As oft as he attempts to hoyst up saile.
>
> 4. 4. 102–03

In an action symbolic as well as practical, she comandeers
those sails and other tackle, and then speaks words which need
some teasing out.

> Are these the sailes that in despight of me
> Packt with the windes to bear *Æneas* hence?
> Ile hang ye in the chamber where I lye.
> Drive if you can my house to *Italy*:
> Ile set the casement open that the windes
> May enter in, and once againe conspire
> Against the life of me poore Carthage Queene:
> But though he goe, he stayes in Carthage still,
> And let rich Carthage fleete upon the seas,
> So I may have *Æneas* in mine armes.
>
> 4. 4. 126–35

These last two lines are clearly echoed in Edward II's words (see above, p. 53). It may seem that the manic fantasies of these two beleaguered characters will bear little interrogation, but there is deep significance in their fantasies.

Dido is driven by her fear that the call of Italy will be too strong for Aeneas and that he will desert her. So, with his sails in her chamber (the sails she provided for him), the chamber—and the palace—and Carthage as well—will become a ship sailing on the sea carrying the two of them to Italy. This is the only way her love and Aeneas' wanderlust can be combined. And if it could happen, she would accept the uprooting of self and kingdom. This sort of rhetoric is meaningless and empty, and immensely pitiable. Its absurdity demonstrates the absolute impossibility of accommodating the inland with the exotic.

Edward, on the other hand, is not trying as Dido is to accommodate and reconcile two impossibly conflicting pressures. His relationship with Gaveston is safe; the affection is mutual. Dido wants protection against her lover's inconstancy; Edward wants protection against those who would divorce him from his lover. So:

> Ere my sweete *Gaveston* shall part from me,
> This Ile shall fleete upon the Ocean,
> And wander to the unfrequented Inde.

If they try to force a separation he will uproot the kingdom and float it into far-off seas to make a Pitcairn Island for himself and Gaveston. Again the force of the fantasy is its absurdity, a play of the mind bespeaking fear and desperation. His quandary is insoluble except in terms of legends of floating islands.

The play of *Dido* is almost entirely about Aeneas' arrival by sea, and the issue of his departure by sea. Voyaging is constantly moving between the literal and the figurative. The involvement of the gods, which is fundamental in Virgil, is for Marlowe, in the end, only decoration. The sea is the great

force, with its archetypal symbolic power, and the seafarer is
the image of man as exile and wanderer, seeking a promised
destination he can never define, driven in and out of havens,
never fully reponsible for his losses and gains. As Stephen
Greenblatt recognized, Aeneas provides an early example of
the 'transcendental homelessness' of Marlowe's heroes,[4] and it
is the sea that makes him what he is.

*   *   *   *   *

> Welcome, great *Bashaws*, how fares *Callymath*?
> What wind drives you thus into *Malta* rode?
> > *Jew of Malta*, 3. 5. 1–2

The Jew of Malta is from beginning to end an island play, with
comings and goings by sea. It is thus linked to the two plays
we have been discussing. But what has happened to the sea?
We have moved from an emblem of separation to an emblem
of desire. The sea has become a servant, a means of extending
and expanding the self. The play's real links are with *Tamburlaine* and *Faustus*. The brilliant introduction, in which Barabas
first soliloquizes and then receives news of his argosies from
his returning merchants, is one long hymn to the appetite for
the wide world's riches. It moves from the low-key account-
ancy of its opening line—'So that of thus much that returne
was made'—to its peak in the vision of 'infinite riches in a little
room'—which may well as G. K. Hunter argued[5] set itself up
in opposition to a very different concept of riches, 'Immensity
cloystered in thy dear womb', as Donne put it.

Like Faustus, Barabas disdains the ambitions of others,
'vulgar trade' producing 'paltry silverlings', and seeks a far
outshining glory.

> Bags of fiery *Opals*, *Saphires*, *Amatists*,
> *Jacints*, hard *Topas*, grasse-greene *Emeraulds*,

---

4 Greenblatt, pp. 194, 196.
5 In 'The Theology of Marlowe's *The Jew of Malta*', Hunter, pp. 75–
80.

Beauteous *Rubyes*, sparkling *Diamonds*,
And seldsene costly stones of so great price . . .
1. 1. 25–28

This concentrate of wealth is an exotic. It has to be fetched
home by ships.

Thine Argosie from *Alexandria*,
Know *Barabas*, doth ride in *Malta* rode,
Laden with riches, and exceeding store
Of *Persian* silkes, of gold, and Orient Perle.
1. 1. 85–88

Thus trowles our fortune in by land and Sea . . .
What more may Heaven doe for earthly man
Then thus to powre out plenty in their laps,
Ripping the bowels of the earth for them,
Making the Sea their servant, and the winds
To drive their substance with successfull blasts?
1. 1. 102, 106–10

This is the ultimate credo of those who see monetary gain as
glory, as the poetry of life and the key to political power.
Voyages bringing back the riches of a new-found world are
essential in the figured tapestry which Marlowe weaves to
body forth the strivings of Tamburlaine and Faustus. Tamburlaine—on the way up—foresees his ships circling the earth,
'Sailing along the Orientall sea . . . / Even from *Persepolis* to
Mexico, / And thence unto the straightes of *Jubalter*' (Part 1;
3. 3. 253–56). Here he seems to think of cutting the Panama
canal, as when he is dying he tells us he had meant to cut the
Suez canal (see the passage at the head of this chapter). He
fetches troops from the ends of the earth, where the ocean
beats on regions 'that never sea-man yet discovered' (Part 2; 1.
1. 71). His global ambitions as he expressed them at the start—

Measuring the limits of his Emperie
By East and west, as *Phœbus* doth his course—
Part 1; 1. 2. 39–40

later take on a remarkable shape. He says he will 'confute . . .
blind Geographers'; he will extend the known regions of the
world and bring them within his control, 'And with this pen
reduce them to a Map' (Part 1; 4. 4. 80).[6]

The dreams of Dr Faustus are in the form of voyages of
discovery and trade.

> Ile have them flye to *India* for gold,
> Ransacke the Ocean for orient pearle,
> And search all corners of the new found world
> For pleasant fruites and princely delicates.
>
> A 114–17

The *Oxford English Dictionary* indicates that 'ransack' could
be used as a fairly neutral term for a very thorough search, but
from medieval times it was associated with violence and
plunder. In his intoxicated vision about the future that lies
before their necromantic team, Valdes lists what their servant-
spirits will do for them.

> From *Venice* shall they dragge huge *Argosies*,
> And from *America* the golden fleece,
> That yearely stuffes olde *Philips* treasury.
>
> A 163–65 (with emendations from B)

The most tantalizing allusion to voyaging in *Faustus* is the
single line, 'He now is gone to proove *Cosmography*'. This
follows the hero's efforts to learn the secrets of astronomy
from the summit of Mount Olympus, where he was taken by a
chariot drawn by dragons. The line is followed in the A-text
(816–18), by the bathetic 'And as I guesse, wil first arive at
Rome, / To see the Pope'. The B-text fills out this abruptness
with a fuller version, with details of Faustus' weariness, which
is too moralistic to be wholly convincing. It supplies an extra
line that seems very obvious.

6 On this passage, see the comments of Gillies, pp. 56–57, and
Greenblatt, p. 198.

He now is gone to prove *Cosmography*,
That measures costs, and kingdomes of the earth:
And as I guesse will first arrive at *Rome*,
To see the Pope . . .

We can accept the substance of the B-text that Faustus made an
aerial tour of the heavens in eight days in his dragon-drawn
chariot, and then set out again on an aerial tour to survey the
surface of the earth—no doubt like Tamburlaine reducing it to
a map, accomplishing in days what it took real voyagers
centuries to do.

Faustus' motives and aspirations are as mixed and confused
as his activities—and the texts that have recorded them—but
what the Evil Angel so largely offers him at the beginning
embraces them all.

Go forward *Faustus* in that famous art,
Wherein all natures treasury is containd:
Be thou on earth as *Jove* is in the skie,
Lord and commaunder of these Elements.
                         A 106–09

Stephen Greenblatt began his memorable essay, 'Marlowe
and the Will to Absolute Play',[7] with a contemporary account
describing gratuitous violence against an African village in
1586 during a voyage set out by the Earl of Cumberland. He
went on as follows.

If, on returning to England in 1587, the merchant and his
associates had gone to see the Lord Admiral's Men
perform a new play, *Tamburlaine the Great*, they would
have seen an extraordinary meditation on the roots of
their own behavior. For despite all the exoticism in
Marlowe—Scythian shepherds, Maltese Jews, German

7 Greenblatt, pp. 193–221; it was first published, in a shorter version, as
'Marlowe and Renaissance Self-Fashioning' in 1977 (in *Two Renaissance
Mythmakers*, ed. Alvin Kernan).

magicians—it is his own countrymen that he broods upon
and depicts . . . If we want to understand the historical
matrix of Marlowe's achievement, the analogue to Tamburlaine's restlessness, aesthetic sensitivity, appetite, and
violence, we might look not at the playwright's literary
sources, not even at the relentless power-hunger of Tudor
absolutism, but at the acquisitive energies of English
merchants, entrepreneurs, and adventurers, promoters
alike of trading companies and theatrical companies.

It could hardly be better put. What form does Marlowe's
'extraordinary meditation' take? Greenblatt's essay, one of the
best pieces of writing on Marlowe in the twentieth century, in
the end heads in the wrong direction, forgetting all about the
voyagers.[8]

For Greenblatt, the heroes of Marlowe's plays are forever
engaged in temporary expedients to create meaning in a
meaningless world, reconstituting themselves and their world
by 'a network of fictions'. Language is an essential part of the
process by which they create themselves, and so is their
violence. They must 'posit an object' and 'pursue a goal' in
order to exist. But all these projects are illusions: Marlowe
suspects that 'all objects of desire are fictions, theatrical
illusions shaped by human subjects' (p. 218). These fictions
are rendered desirable by 'the intoxication of language, by the
will to play'. The enterprises of all the heroes are 'at once
necessary and absurd', their lives a struggle against 'the
nothingness' into which they fall at the end of each play
(p. 200).

Marlowe himself, Greenblatt maintained, is 'deeply implic-
ated in his heroes'. As a writer filled with contempt for the
ethics and absolutes of his society, his activity, as man and
dramatist, is—play: 'play on the brink of an abyss, *absolute*
play'. He invents fictions too, fashions lines 'that echo in the

---

8 See my reviews in *The Yearbook of English Studies*, 1981, pp. 244–45,
and *Renaissance Quarterly*, 1982, pp. 317–21.

void, that echo more powerfully because there is nothing but a void' (pp. 220–21).

The true goal of all Marlowe's heroes, Greenblatt wrote, 'is to be characters in Marlowe's plays' (p. 221). It would have been very helpful if at the conclusion of his essay Greenblatt had returned to the voyagers and adventurers with whom he began in order to confirm that the plays, as he had now described them, were indeed 'an extraordinary meditation on the roots of their own behaviour'. Suppose we look at the final and fatal enterprises of four Elizabethan and Jacobean adventurers, Humphrey Gilbert, Thomas Cavendish, Henry Hudson, and Walter Ralegh.[9] It is very instructive to ask how the careers of these men could, and how they could not, be fitted into Greenblatt's pattern. Each of them was lured by a vision of fame, wealth and power and destroyed himself and many others in its pursuit. Gilbert wanted to be the ruler of a huge British empire in North America; Cavendish wanted to be the first man to sail round the world twice and to open up trade in the fabulous East; Hudson wanted to reach the same market by finding the North-West Passage; Ralegh wanted to find the gold of Guiana to rehabilitate his ruined fortunes. There is something intensely Marlovian about the grandeur of their dreams and the wretchedness of the attempted realization, and there is much in their efforts to mould themselves (and those whom they persuaded to follow them) into the contours of their high projects which fits what Greenblatt describes.

But how far can we describe their attitudes and activities as play? Certainly there was something intrinsically histrionic about their self-portrayal, and it is also true their careers followed a pattern which Elizabethan theatregoers would have recognized as tragic. But they were not characters in a play. On the contrary, their role in pursuing their dreams was to carry out practice-runs for those who in succeeding gener-

9 These are examined in Edwards (1988) and (1992).

ations stamped the formidable reality of the British Empire all over the world. Their aspirations may have started as self-constituting fictions, but that is only half the story. The other half is how those fictions became a very dark reality for many peoples all over the world. Ralegh began a well-known poem: 'What is our life? a play of passion'. It ends like this:

> Thus march we playing to our latest rest,
> Onely we dye in earnest, that's no Jest.[10]

The tragic paradigm of Marlowe's plays, like that of Shakespeare's *Macbeth*, is the conversion of fantasy into reality. ('Who would have thought the olde man to have had so much blood in him?') The summation of Marlowe's vision is the career of Faustus, who sold his soul because otherwise 'mine owne fantasie . . . will receive no object for my head' (A 136–37).   It was not the destiny of Marlowe's heroes to end up in a play. Their role was to be prophets of the twentieth century, which is as real as can be. The unending tragedy of the world's history since 1590, including the slave-trade, the genocide of the native inhabitants of North America, the holocaust, the different forms of massacre, torture and terror going on as I write this in Indonesia, Africa, Latin America, China, the Balkans and other parts of the world, is not, in any definition, play. Marlowe's vision was not of emptiness, not of nothingness, but of the fulness of time. The play of his heroes, and his own plays, became inexorable reality.

It was the truest part of Greenblatt's essay that Marlowe's great rebels against society were in fact supporters of society's deepest values. Marlowe had nothing but contempt for the sanctimonious hypocrisy and humbug of those who oppose Tamburlaine and Barabas. Everyone in Malta wants the riches that Barabas openly lusts for, and is prepared to be as machiavellian as he is. Barabas was their spokesman. Tamburlaine, Barabas and Faustus were the spearhead of modern

10 *Poems*, ed. Latham (1951) pp. 51–52.

western culture, and Marlowe could see both its glory and its horror.

It had to be by means of voyaging that Europe enriched itself by trade and conquest. And, as Bacon knew, voyaging was an integral factor in the acquisition of the knowledge by which western man became 'lord and commander' of the elements. The image of the voyage was indispensable in Marlowe's prophetic plays. Indispensable in his picture of the subjugation of the world's territories and peoples in *Tamburlaine,* and in his picture of global capitalism in the first act of *The Jew of Malta.* It is not so much to the fore in the picture of the advance of science and technology in *Dr Faustus,* but it is still there, in talk of proving cosmography, and ransacking the ocean for orient pearl.

Marlowe puts fire, poetry, even majesty into the aspirations and the longings of his heroes, and he charts the degeneration of each one of them into sterility. There is not one of those heroes whose aspirations at their most ardent and lyrical are not fatally flawed. Can any one of them withstand the parody of their dreams given to the slave Ithamore in *The Jew of Malta* as he entices the courtesan Bellamira?

> We will leave this paltry land,
> And saile from hence to *Greece,* to lovely *Greece,*
> I'le be thy *Jason,* thou my golden Fleece;
> Where painted Carpets o're the meads are hurl'd,
> And *Bacchus* vineyards ore-spread the world;
> Where Woods and Forrests goe in goodly greene,
> I'le be *Adonis,* thou shalt be Loves Queene.
> The Meads, the Orchards, and the Primrose lanes,
> Instead of Sedge and Reed, beare Sugar Canes:
> Thou in those Groves, by *Dis* above,
> Shalt live with me and be my love.
>
> 4. 2. 94–104

The poetry of the expanding self—widely regarded as Marlowe's greatest achievement—is here exposed in the tawdry glitter which always threatens to replace its lustre. It is never unchallenged, even at its greatest, because Ithamore, the Doppelgänger of them all, makes his presence felt in the finest speeches of the towering heroes.

* * * * *

The two contrasting images in Marlowe's plays of the sea and the voyage, as emblem of separation and as emblem of desire, seem opposed and incompatible. They project antithetical views of the self, one passive and receptive, the other active and acquisitive; one a needy thing protected within palisades, the other struggling against confines and roaming restlessly towards fulfilment. Dido and Edward II wait by the edge of the sea; what lies beyond is utterly mysterious, a region of danger and threat, yet the sea is also the route by which love comes and by which it departs. In the world of *Tamburlaine*, *The Jew of Malta*, *Dr Faustus*, the sea is servant to the hero, the route to the unknown which is waiting to be possessed, tamed and exploited. The sea is a pathway to extend the self into almost unimaginable dimensions of power. This quest for self-fulfilment ends in self– destruction, however—not least in *Tamburlaine*, in which the insane obsession of the hero in his role as scourge of God is a subtler portrayal of disintegration than the black farce of the death of Barabas.

Thus there is an antagonism within each of the two antagonistic perceptions. To the victim the sea brings love but also danger; for the adventurer the sea is the avenue both to the enlargement of the self and to the desiccation of the spirit. The two images are neither alternatives nor rivals; they are partners. In *The Faerie Queene*, the equivocation of the voyage metaphor displayed life in the contrasting modes of determined endeavour and patient expectation. In Marlowe's plays it projects two complementary versions of the human spirit, each with its own form of the divided self, longing and fear in the one, exhilaration and bitterness in the other. All this is within the resources of imagery of the sea. If Marlowe's plays have become myths of modern existence, it is partly because the metaphor of the voyage, with him as with Spenser, proves a potent instrument for revealing the conflicting impulses and urges which dominate more than a single age.

CHAPTER THREE—DONNE
'Is the Pacifique Sea my home?'

Since I am comming to that Holy roome,
    Where, with thy Quire of Saints for evermore,
I shall be made thy Musique; As I come
    ' I tune the Instrument here at the dore,
    And what I must doe then, thinke now before.

Whilst my Physitians by their love are growne
    Cosmographers, and I their Mapp, who lie
Flat on this bed, that by them may be showne
    That this is my South-west discoverie
    Per fretum febris, by these streights to die,

I joy, that in these straits, I see my West;
    For, though theire currants yeeld returne to none,
What shall my West hurt me? As West and East
    In all flatt Maps (and I am one) are one,
    So death doth touch the Resurrection.

Is the Pacifique Sea my home? Or are
    The Easterne riches? Is *Jerusalem*?
Anyan, and *Magellan*, and *Gibraltare*,
    All streights, and none but streights, are wayes to them,
    Whether where *Japhet* dwelt, or *Cham*, or *Sem*.

We thinke that *Paradise* and *Calvarie*,
    Christs Crosse, and *Adams* tree, stood in one place;
Looke Lord, and finde both *Adams* met in me;
    As the first *Adams* sweat surrounds my face,
    May the last *Adams* blood my soule embrace.

So, in his purple wrapp'd receive mee Lord,
    By these his thornes give me his other Crowne;

And as to others soules I preach'd thy word,
  Be this my Text, my Sermon to mine owne,
  Therfore that he may raise the Lord throws down.[1]

John Donne's serious illness of 1623 was the occasion of two
major poems, the 'Hymne to God my God, in my sicknesse',
above,[2] and 'A Hymne to God the Father' (see p. 95), as well
as the prose work, *Devotions upon Divergent Occasions*. All
three writings make central use of voyage imagery, the
'Hymne to God my God' being entirely dependent on it. My
study of Donne's voyage imagery as a whole will lead up to an
examination of this difficult and challenging poem.

Unlike Spenser's, Donne's references to voyaging, which
are everywhere in his writing and constitute some of its best-
known moments, directly invoke the contemporary world.
'Oh my America, my new found lande!'

  Let sea-discoverers to new worlds have gone,
  Let Maps to others, worlds on worlds have showne,
  Let us possesse our world, each hath one, and is one.

  In what torne ship soever I embarke,
  That ship shall be my embleme of thy Arke.

In this last couplet, Donne was reflecting on his forthcoming
journey to Germany in 1619. Two important poems, 'The
Storme' and 'The Calme', and a number of epigrams, are based

---

1 Quotations from Donne's writings are taken from the following
editions: the Elegies and the Songs and Sonnets from Helen Gardner's
Oxford edition of 1965; the Divine Poems from her edition of 1952; Satires,
Epigrams and Verse Letters from Wesley Milgate's Oxford edition of 1967.
Other poems from Herbert Grierson's edition in the Oxford Standard
format, 1933 etc. Sermons from the Potter and Simpson edition, 10
volumes, University of California Press, 1953–59; Devotions from Anthony
Raspa's edition, McGill-Queen's University Press, 1975.
2 On the dating of this poem, see Helen Gardner in *Divine Poems*,
Appendix E.

on his actual experiences at sea during the expedition to Cadiz and the Islands voyage in 1596–97.[3]

Many of Donne's sea-images had a long life. One of his favourites was the image of ballast. In 'Aire and Angels', love is a pinnace, and the speaker thinks to ballast it and go more steadily with 'thy lip, eye, and brow'. But that makes the pinnace 'overfraught'. In a letter to Sir Henry Goodyer (1608?), Donne wrote that he had 'cast out all my ballast which nature and time gives, Reason and discretion, . . . but I have over fraught my self with Vice . . .'[4] In *The Second Anniversary* (1612), he wrote that 'so much knowledge, as would over– fraight / Another, did but ballast her' (lines 316–17). In his sermons, from 1617 onwards, ballast and freight are constants. The ballast of the soul is purity, or cheerfulness, or humility, or social duty, or love of God. This ballast, which keeps the ship steady and prevents it from capsizing and sinking, is often also the ship's cargo, the freight it carries to the heavenly haven: 'Keep up that holy cheerefulnesse, which Christ makes the Ballast of a Christian, and his Fraight too, to give him a riche Returne in the Heavenly Jerusalem'.[5] Two other images, which, like ballast and freight, recur throughout Donne's writing are the image of the flat map of the world (so important in the 'Hymne to God my God'), and the image of the north star—which is only an approximation to true north.

With voyaging as with all knowledge and experience, Donne is equally at home with old and new, ancient and modern, and will play one against the other. He relishes the authority of the traditional and time-honoured tropes of the sea, but many of his voyage images are quite unexpected and newly thought-out, using specific knowledge personally acquired—by reading if not by experience. Although he constantly uses the story of Jonah and the whale, he can also

3 A number of relevant images are cited in Rugoff's book, *Donne's Imagery*, section XII, 'Sea Travel and Exploration'.

4 Nonesuch Donne, ed. J. Hayward (1929), p. 450.

5 *Sermons*, vii, p. 440.

create metaphor out of the most up-to-date information on current whaling techniques, as in one of the sermons for the Countess of Bridgwater (1621 or 1623).

> The rebuke of sin, is like the fishing of *Whales*; the Marke is great enough; one can scarce misse hitting; but if there be not *sea room* and line enough, and a dexterity in letting out that line, he that hath fixed his harping Iron, in the Whale, endangers himselfe, and his boate; God hath made us *fishers of Men;* and when we have struck a *Whale,* touch'd the conscience of any person, which thought himselfe above rebuke, and increpation, it struggles, and strives, and as much as it can, endevours to draw fishers, and boate, the Man and his fortune into contempt, and danger. But if God tye a *sicknesse,* or any other calamity, to the end of the line, that will winde up this Whale againe, to the boate, bring back this rebellious sinner better advised, to the mouth of the Minister, for more counsaile . . .[6]

Everyone must know the draught of his own vessel, said Donne the preacher, and not think that because another ship has got over his can as well. Again, he who gives up all sins but one 'is in no better case, then if at Sea he should stop all leaks but one, and perish by that'. In a sermon of 1623, in an extended passage of seafaring imagery, Donne spoke of three stages of the sea, before, during and after a storm, to indicate three spiritual conditions: first, false security, secondly, 'a remorseless stupefaction', and thirdly, the troubled mind, when 'the danger is past, but yet the billow is great still'.[7] In another sermon, he described how in the worst of storms at sea, the sailors will cut down galleries and cabins to ease the ship, and even the mast itself, 'but no foule weather can make

6 *Ibid.*, v, p. 199–200.
7 *Ibid.*, vi, p. 58–59; the two previous references are to iv, p. 329, and to ix, p. 267.

them tear out the keele of the ship'. So the church, 'in cases of necessity', can dispense with 'the super-edifications of men', but 'to the *keele* of the *ship*, to the *fundamentall articles* of Religion', no violence is to be offered: and she must 'be content to *hull* it out . . . during the storme'.[8]

A great many of the voyages which Donne brings into service, in his poetry as well as in his sermons, are trading voyages; and such voyages introduce a major question about the valuations which stem from maritime conjunctions and similitudes. Do we allow ourselves our discomfort with the commercialism, the devotional capitalism, of the passage I have already cited, in which 'holy cheerfulnesse', the ballast and freight of a Christian, will 'give him a rich Returne in the Heavenly Jerusalem'? Or do we say that our modern liberal consciences are interfering with less troubled renaissance responses? The correspondences are very frequent. For example: as international commerce joins distant nations together, so mercy reconciles things that are asunder. As a merchant can see the rough seas ahead of him, but can't see the commodities (i.e., profits) he is out to win, so we can see our troubles, but not our heavenly reward. Investing, or becoming a venturer, in a trading voyage, is a frequent parallel for the life of devotion. The oddest of them, perhaps, is that *not* to become an adventurer in an East-Indian enterprise leaves you no poorer than before, though you are not richer; but not to take comfort in the Holy Ghost is to suffer 'an extraordinary condemnation', because the offer was an 'extraordinary favour'.[9]

In the poem, 'To Mr. Tilman after he had taken orders', there is a very interesting depreciation of commerce in comparison with the life of the spirit, which actually places a high romantic value on trading enterprises even as it denies them the highest rank. This simile does not really form an

8 *Ibid.*, x, p. 109.
9 *Ibid.*, v, pp. 238, 215; vii, 439.

exception; the language of spiritual commitment is still that of
'trafficking'; but it is a warning of how quickly the currency of
Donne's sea-metaphors can change value.

> Or, as a Ship after much paine and care,
> For Iron and Cloth brings home rich Indian ware,
> Hast thou thus traffiqu'd, but with farre more gaine
> Of noble goods, and with lesse time and paine?

It is axiomatic that the function of the Metaphysical
comparison was to confer quality rather than to delineate or
measure. (As when, in 'A Valediction: forbidding Mourning',
separated souls endure not a breach but an expansion, 'Like
gold to ayery thinnesse beate'.) The grant of quality in a simile
is a reciprocal business: each arm of the simile is busy
transmitting honour or dishonour to its fellow. In a universe
of unfixed and varying values, the moment two things are
compared, they each start trembling with uncertainty. It is not
our embarrassment alone that in Donne's poetry and sermons
holy matters are described in unholy terms; it is Donne's
embarrassment too. Mercantile enterprises do not for him
have a fixed value of high romance and shining reward. Insofar
as he can sometimes view them with a sceptical eye, their value
ceases to be sacrosanct, and similes which employ them to
venerate spiritual endeavour risk diminishing that endeavour.
Here, from a sermon, is a powerful challenge to the idea of a
merchant's 'rich Indian ware' as a suitable equivalent for
spiritual reward.

> I must not think to *bribe* God, by giving him some of the
> profit of my sinne, to let me enjoy the rest: for, was God a
> *venturer* with me in my sinne? Or did God set me to Sea,
> that is, put me into this world, to see what I could get by
> *Usury*, by *Oppression*, by *Extortion*, and then give him a
> part to *charitable uses*?[10]

Here is another one.

10 *Ibid.*, vi, p. 200.

Even whilest your money is under your fingers, whilest it is in your purposes determined, and digested for such, and such a purpose, whilest you have put it in a ship in Merchandice, to win more to it; whilest you have sow'd it in the land of borrowers, to multiply, and grow upon Mortgages, and usury, even when you are in the mid'st of your travail, stormes at Sea, theeves at land, enviers at court, informations at *Westminster*, whilest the meat is in your mouthes, shall cast the wrath of God upon your riches, and they shall perish, *In occupatione*, then, when you travail to increase them.[11]

Seafaring matters in Donne's writings vary greatly in what they can be used for and applied to as metaphors. They are also equivocal and contradictory in the value they impart to what they are charged to clarify and illuminate.

* * * * *

There is an impressive examination and demonstration by Donne of his methods and motives in using metaphors from the sea in the nineteenth section of his *Devotions upon Emergent Occasions,* written during his severe illness in 1623. His illness has passed its peak; the bad or morbific matter which has been plaguing him has ripened, or concocted as he puts it, and is now ready for elimination as a cloudy substance in his urine, spittle, or other excretion. The section is headed thus: '*At last, the Physitians, after a long and stormie voyage, see land; They have so good signes of the concoction of the disease, as that they may safely proceed to purge*'.

In the preliminary meditation, this figure is as it were fortified. The physicians have been 'patiently attending when they should see any *land* in this *Sea,* any *earth,* any *cloud,* any *indication* of *concoction* in these *waters*'. The water is Donne's water; and the land or cloud they look for is the cloudy

11 *Ibid.,* iii, p. 63.

substance in his urine. In the 'expostulation' which follows, Donne justifies his curious imagery in an invocation to a God who, besides being a literal God, is '*a figurative*, a *metaphoricall God*'. Such a description, writes Donne, is intended to God's glory, and must not be misinterpreted as a diminution. God is metaphorical not only in his words, but in his works. 'The *stile* of thy *works*, the *phrase* of thine *Actions*, is *Metaphoricall.*' Under the old law, '*figures* flowed into *figures*, and powred themselves out into *farther figures*'. For example, circumcision was a figure of baptism, and baptism a figure of the purity we shall have in heaven. This continued in the time of Christ. 'How often, how much more often doth thy *Sonne* call himselfe a *way*, and a *light*, and a *gate*, and a *Vine*, and *bread*, than the *Sonne of God*, or of *Man*? How much oftner doth he exhibit a *Metaphoricall Christ* than a *reall*, a *literall*?'

Because God spoke in figures, his ancient servants spoke in figures, in their public liturgies and private prayers. 'In which manner I am bold to call the comfort which I receive now in this sicknesse, in the *indication* of the *concoction* and *maturity* thereof, in certaine *clouds*, and *residences*, which the *Physitians* observe, a discovering of *land* from *Sea*, after a long, and tempestuous *voyage*.' He then asks why God should choose waters as a metaphor for the afflictions and calamities of life. Is it because we are to be drowned in a bottomless and boundless sea? No. 'Thats not the *dialect* of thy *language*; thou hast given a *Remedy* against the deepest *water*, by *water*; against the *inundation* of sinne, by *Baptisme*.' So the word is set against the word, or rather the figure against the figure. A single symbol may be the host to wholly opposed connotations.

There are also other means by which God counters the threatening signification of the sea. 'What is our *refuge*? thine *Arke*, thy *ship*.' In the sea of Donne's sickness, God's ship is his physician. God, however, may not work directly; he may prefer to work through 'means'. In the case of this sickness, through physicians: and the physicians are Donne's immediate ship. 'But as they are *Ships* to us in those *Seas*, so is there a *Ship* to them too, in which they are to stay.' Their ship is their religious faith.

In a ship within a ship, Donne asks what assurance he has of God's mercy.

> What is my *seale*? It is but a *cloud*; that which my *Physitians* call a *cloud*, is *that*, which gives them their *Indication*. But a *Cloud*? Thy *great Seale* to all the world, the *raine-bow*, that secured the *world* for ever, from *drowning*, was but a *reflexion upon a cloud*. A *cloud* it selfe was a *pillar* which guided the *church*, and *the glory of God* not only *was*, but *appeared in a cloud* ... *Seven dayes*, O my *God*, have we looked for this *cloud*, and now we have it; none of thy *Indications* are *frivolous*; thou makest thy *signes, seales;* and thy *Seales, effects* ... [12]

It is a tortuous argument, and one may worry about a concept of salvation that depends upon the identity of the word used by the physician for thickish matter in urine and the cloud arising from the sea which promised rain to Elijah. But 'none of thy *Indications* are *frivolous*; thou makest thy *signes, seales*'.

Nevertheless, indications, if not frivolous, are ambivalent, equivocal, polysemous. The sea which indicates calamity and affliction also indicates baptism. In fact, the sea was used by Donne as a sign of very many other things as well. Frequently, it is Christ's blood; but it is also the blood of the martyrs. On other occasions, it is the scriptures, the church, God's mercy. These are its better acceptations. The sea is also commination and judgement, the inconstancy of people, uncharitableness, and (in a recurrent pun) the sea of Rome. In one sermon an exposition of the various ways in which the world could be regarded as a sea is used as a rhetorical technique.

The sea is not an unalterable, univocal divine symbol. Nor can it be said that all its acceptations are received rather than

12 *Devotions*, pp. 99–103.

given. Signification is chosen. What the sea indicates is what
the mind wills.

> In what torne ship soever I embarke,
> That ship shall be my embleme of thy Arke.

The idea that every material thing pressed in upon Donne as an
emblem of divine presence must give way to a sense of his
determination that all things *should* declare the divine
presence. 'Be covetous of Crosses', he wrote in 'The Crosse'.

> The Mast and yard make one, where seas do tosse.

'None of thy *Indications* are *frivolous*.' This must mean that
nothing that can enter Donne's mind as a possible divine
signification is frivolous.

*   *   *   *   *

The great value of the image of voyaging, indeed its chief
importance, is its usefulness in talking about a purposeful
moral life. This is as true of Donne's work as of Spenser's.
'The world is a Sea . . . in this respect, that the Sea is no place
of habitation, but a passage to our habitations.'[13] Ships are a
means of getting somewhere. 'We see ships in the river', he
said, 'but all their use is gone, if they go not to sea.'[14] In the
sermons, navigating the stormy seas is of course an image of
striving to reach the haven of heaven. Life is constantly a
spiritual voyage, with all the perils of storm, rocks and
shipwreck, and the promise of quiet harbour at last. In
preaching before the king in 1629, he proposed to take his
auditors through 'the whole Compasse of mans voyage, from
his lanching forth in this world, to his Anchoring in the next;
from his hoysing sayle here, to his striking sayle there'. Two
years earlier he had spoken of 'our *Voyage* through this *Sea*,

13 *Sermons*, ii, p. 307.
14 *Ibid.*, ii, 246.

which is truly a *Mediterranean Sea*, a *Sea* betwixt two *Lands*, the *Land* of *Possession*, which wee have, and the *Land* of *Promise*, which wee expect'.[15]

Henry Wotton had been with Donne on both the Cadiz expedition and the Islands voyage in 1596 and 1597. Donne's verse letter to him, 'Sir, more then kisses', is thought to belong to the months after their return—over twenty-five years earlier than any of the sermon passages just quoted. Assuming, as the sermons do, a moral purpose in life, the poem strikingly challenges the suitability and convenience of the life-as-voyage trope which is blandly proclaimed at the outset: 'Life is a voyage . . .' (line 7).

Journeying involves visiting or calling in at places on the way; life as a journey must involve contact with cities, the court, the country; and all these are corrupting. You can't steer clear of them all, and you can't avoid their stain. In order to contrast the incrustations of sin and vice with the innocence of youth, Donne brilliantly re-employs the voyage metaphor he is repudiating and suggests a ship, a long way on in its life-voyage, putting in at an island and discovering a strange race of beings—who are actually the voyagers, when young.

> I thinke if men, which in these places live
> Durst looke for themselves, and themselves retrive,
> They would like strangers greet themselves, seeing then
> Utopian youth, growne old Italian. (43–46)

A new metaphor is required for a life of integrity, since the image of the journey involves unavoidable contamination. ('Inne any where, continuance maketh hell.') A number of possibilities are tried. 'In thy selfe dwell.' Follow the snail, who carries his own house. 'Bee thine own Palace, or the world's thy Gaole.' But the idea that the world *is* a sea can't be defeated, won't go away. The new image for the pure life that emerges is not that of a ship, but that of a fish.

15 *Ibid.*, ix, 68; viii, 64.

And in the worlds sea, do not like corke sleepe
Upon the waters face; nor in the deepe
Sinke like a lead without a line: but as
Fishes glide, leaving no print where they passe,
Nor making sound, so, closely thy course goe. (53–56)[16]

We may be reminded of the reference in the 'Elegie on Mrs Boulstred' to 'the deepe / Where harmelesse fish monastique silence keepe'. The idea of pure life as soundless moving through water is implicit in 'A Valediction: forbidding Mourning': 'So let us melt, and make no noise, / No teare-floods, nor sigh-tempests move'. The idea of trackless movement through water, leaving no print, is transferred to a ship in one of the sermons. The mercy of God retains 'no record against us', 'as the Sea retaines no impression of the Ships that passe in it, (for Navies make no path in the Sea)'.[17]

The basic metaphor of a voyage can be interrogated. It can be shown to be an heuristic failure, or an heuristic success. A quite different confrontation and challenge to the value of the voyage as an image for spiritual life lies in Donne's early use of it in sexual contexts.

Who ever loves, if hee doe not propose
The right true end of love, hee's one which goes
To sea for nothing but to make him sicke.[18]

If the right true end of a voyage is the haven of sexual intercourse, it is still possible to take an unwise route.

And sailing towards her India, in that way
Shall at her faire Atlantique navell stay;
Though thence the currant be thy pilot made,

16 'closely' means 'secretly'.
17 *Sermons*, v, p. 318; in *Wisdom of the Ancients*, section IV ('Narcissus'), Bacon uses the image of a ship's passage that leaves no trace in the water to illustrate a useless and fruitless life; cf. also Jonson's masque, *Neptunes Triumph*, Herford and Simpson, vii, p. 697.
18 'Loves Progress'.

Yet ere thou bee where thou wouldst bee embay'd,
Thou shalt upon another forrest set
Where some doe shipwracke, and no farther gett.

The amatory voyage may have a different *telos*. In 'Confined Love', the image of voyages of discovery and trade is used to argue the rightness of regularly changing sexual partners.

Who e'r rigg'd faire ship to lie in harbors,
And not to seeke new lands, or not to deale withall?

Helen Gardner thought that 'Confined Love' was spoken by a woman. Ships are traditionally female, as they are occupied by men; but traditionally male as they penetrate new lands.

What effect does this secular and sexual use of the voyage image have on the prestige of voyaging? Time and again, throughout Donne's writings, both the East and the West Indies are evoked as symbols of all that is precious and most desirable—'two rich and fragrant fields . . . the Western Hemispheare, the land of Gold, and Treasure, and the Eastern Hemispheare, the land of Spices and Perfumes'. In this passage[19] the gold represents the 'Essentiall goodnesse in God himself', and the spices and perfumes 'the dilatation of Gods goodnesse'. I have suggested that the materialism of trading for these precious goods confers no favour on the spiritual values they are identified with. How much further are spiritual values compromised by the use of these symbols of what is most precious to glorify the quest for sexual gratification?

In 'The Sunne Rising' Donne writes that 'both the India's of spice and Myne . . . lie here with mee'. The underlying pun in 'mine' brings in the note of triumphant possessiveness which dominates the use of voyage imagery in the love poems. 'The woman may become the world . . . but she is a world owned and ruled, indeed, rifled and exploited', wrote John Carey.[20]

19 *Ibid.*, vi, p. 231.
20 Carey, p. 98. Cf. Thomas Healy, *New Latitudes*, London, 1992, pp. 145–46.

In these sexual voyage-similes, both activities, the search for gold and territory on the one hand and sexual conquest on the other, come off badly. In many of the Elegies and the Songs and Sonnets, behind all the banter and extravagant pro-testation, when sex and voyaging are put into a relationship, whether of comparison or contrast, each of them suffers.

> Licence my roving hands, and let them goe
> Behind, before, above, between, below.
> Oh my America, my new found lande,
> My kingdome, safeliest when with one man man'd,
> My myne of precious stones, my Empiree,
> How blest am I in this discovering thee.
> ('To his Mistris Going to Bed', 25–30)

It is impossible to get away from the idea that appropriation, domination, and the demand for exclusive rights are equally involved in both 'discoveries'—of a woman, and of America. Here, as often, love and voyaging are reciprocally cheapened rather than honoured by being brought into relationship. The voyage of discovery, the territory it was supposed to win, and the riches it was supposed to bring back, have to limp into their use as religious symbols with the heavy burden of their past sexual use on their backs.

In writing of the domineering and possessive attitude to women which he quite justly observes in Donne's love poetry, John Carey gives the impression that he is, with some regret, unmasking John Donne's true nature. But this flippant and witty conquest-poetry is only one of the many issues of Donne's capacious and enthusiastic imagination. He must have known what kind of a lover he had created. There is plenty of evidence in Donne's poetry of disapproval of the arrogance of the imperial enterprise, and I assume that he was as aware as we are of the arrogance of the sexual enterprise with which it is compared.

In Satire III, the courage to go to sea for the purpose of obtaining riches is despised as 'courage of straw', the wrong sort of courage in men who fail to understand the true aim of life.

> Hast thou couragious fire to thaw the ice
> Of frozen North discoveries? and thrise
> Colder then Salamanders, like divine
> Children in th'oven, fires of Spaine, and the line,
> Whose countries limbecks to our bodies bee,
> Canst thou for gaine beare? (21–26)

In poetry of such constant hyperbole and advocacy as Donne's, a brew in which the theatrical and the confessional lie fermenting together, it is left to the individual reader to salute those passages which he or she finds more seriously meant. One may give more weight in this respect to the satires than to some of the love poems. 'Loves Warre' protests that no worldly occupation is as important as love, but that is the kind of thing an ardent lover says. It is not so easy to discount the passage scorning voyages to the Spanish Main.

> And Midas joyes our Spanish journeys give,
> Wee touch all gold, but find no foode to live. (18–19)

The damage done by this couplet is immense. It depreciates and devalues the currency used to laud and glorify sex, love, and devotion. There is a clear allusion to Juvenal's tag, 'propter vitam vivendi perdere causas'—so to live as to deny the true purpose of life. Real gold destroys us after our painful search for it. Sexual 'gold' is by implication downgraded in a rhetoric purposing to uplift it.

In that same passage of the elegy, ships are called prisons, and 'carts for executions' (lines 21–22, and 26). And in the passage of Satire III which we have looked at, ships are called 'woodden Sepulchers'. Derogatory images such as these introduce us to the sea-world of 'The Storme' and 'The Calme', the two verse letters which Donne wrote concerning his experiences at sea during the second of his two expeditions, taking part in the 'Islands Voyage' of 1597. Here was an enterprise of

high national importance, aimed at the power of Spain, and
once again Donne had engaged himself as a gentleman volun-
teer, eager no doubt for the excitement as well as service to the
country 'to whom we owe, what we be, and have' ('Storme',
9). The expedition was first thwarted by a violent storm which
scattered the fleet, and later frustrated by a disabling calm. In
Donne's poems, the whole idea of voyage as passage towards a
goal is negated, as all planning, effort and aspiration are
defeated. Elemental visitations convert the expedition into a
journey to the heart of darkness, where all the assumptions
and expectations of civil life vanish.

> And all our beauty, and our trimme, decayes,
> Like courts removing, or like ended playes.
>   ('Calme', 13–14)

The starkness of primordial reality behind the 'frippery' of
normal life is manifest in the darkness accompanying the fury
of the storm.

> But when I wakt, I saw, that I saw not;
> I, and the Sunne, which should teach mee, had forgot
> East, West, Day, Night, and I could but say,
> If the world had lasted, now it had beene day.
>   ('Storme', 37–40)

Cabins are coffins, from which their occupants emerge like
souls from their graves to gaze in fear at a scene of terror.

> And from our totterd sailes, ragges drop downe so,
> As from one hang'd in chaines, a yeare agoe.
>   (*ibid.*, 57–58)

The only light is the lightning, the rain is torrential, and the
noise tumultuous—not only the noise of thunder, but the
noise of rigging 'snapping, like too-high-stretched treble
strings'. The sailors are deafened, but there would be no point
in hearing, because language is no longer operative: 'there's
none knowes what to say'.

This is an existence anterior to the order of God, the state of
Chaos, which Milton too saw in the image of storm—

—the vast immeasurable Abyss
Outrageous as a Sea, dark, wasteful, wilde,
Up from the bottom turnd by furious windes
And surging waves, as Mountains to assault
Heav'ns highth, and with the Center mix the Pole.
(*Paradise Lost*, vii, 211–15)

Everything recognizable has dissolved into shapelessness, and
'uniforme deformity' reigns—

—so that wee, except God say
Another *Fiat*, shall have no more day.
('Storme', 71–72)

The storm has provided an image of what lies behind the stage-
scenery of what we consider to be reality. We are in fact in a
state in which God's order no longer prevails, and a new
revelation of His power is required—a new creation, indeed.

Commentators on 'The Storme' point to the importance of
the allusions to Sarah and to Jonah, both of them blessed by
the miraculous intervention of God. Clayton D. Lein believes
that the allusion to Jonah 'expresses the ultimate theme of the
poem' and 'becomes the key embodiment of Donne's personal
vision of salvation'.[21] L. Mizejewski is more cautious. There is
'a strong sense of religious perplexity in the poem', but, as
regards Sarah and Jonah, 'the impact of God's presence is felt
in the terror of pre-creation chaos'.[22] She makes the important
point that, though in 'The Storme' the speaker goes no further
than to trust that the universe is still in God's hands, the
companion poem, 'The Calme', has even less confidence, and
is a more pessimistic poem.

'The Calme' opens with a reference to the fable of the frogs

21 Lein, p. 160.
22 Mizejewski, p. 224.

and the stork: the frogs asked God for a king and were given a log; they objected, so they were given a stork, who gobbled them up. The Englishmen were sent a storm, and prayed for a calm; they got it, and their suffering is worse. And 'Heaven laughs to see us languish thus'. The poem is about the vanity of human wishes, the powerlessness of men to achieve the ends they desire. Stuck in this flat calm, the Englishmen are incapable of moving in any direction. They cannot do the fighting they came out to do; they cannot even move. The 'fighting-place', indeed, has become an old-clothes shop, with the sailors' washing hung out to dry. As in the other poem, all expectations are inverted. When they bathe they are not refreshed.

The calm is an image of the impotence of humankind. But the frustration which paralyses us is as much our responsibility as it is the result of the caprice of fortune or the indifference of the gods.

> And on the hatches as on Altars lyes
> Each one, his owne Priest, and owne Sacrifice.
> Who live, that miracle do multiply
> Where walkers in hot Ovens, doe not dye.
> ('Calme', 25–28)

As with the frogs, we bring our suffering upon ourselves, our vain wishes being fed into a system operated by a grudging fate, which 'doth subtly lay / A scourge, 'gainst which wee all forget to pray'. Failure to achieve his end leads Donne to examine his own motives in volunteering, and now he finds them suspect.

> Whether a rotten state, and hope of gaine,
> Or to disuse mee from the queasie paine
> Of being belov'd, and loving, or the thirst
> Of honour, or faire death, out pusht mee first,
> I lose my end.
> (*ibid.*, 39–43)

'What are wee then?', the poem ends by asking. 'How little more alas / Is man now, then before he was?' Before the creation he was—nothing. (We have gone back to the pre–Creation chaos of the ending of 'The Storme'.) And now?

> Wee are for nothing fit;
> Chance, or our selves still disproportion it.
> (*ibid.*, 54–55)

A voyage frustrated of its purpose of harrying the Spaniards by a calm has become an image of a life lacking order and meaning. 'Disproportion', or the lack of meaningful shape, is the fault of our own mixed motives and questionable purposes as well as the malignity of fate or fortune.

The vision of paralysis in 'The Calme', in which each one is 'his owne Priest, and owne Sacrifice', makes the poem even more impressive than 'The Storme', with its apocalyptic vision of a return to chaos. Like 'The Storme', 'The Calme' has its biblical reference, this time to Shadrach, Meshack, and Abednego, the 'walkers in hot Ovens', saved by miracle. At times the biblical references in the two poems appear to work negatively, like invocations and allusions in *The Waste Land* to a richer and more fruitful life which only confirm and emphasize current sterility and deprivation. The possibility that this allusion to Shadrach, Meshack, and Abednego could be ironic is strengthened by the flippant reference to the 'divine / Children in th'oven' in Satire III (see above). At best, the biblical allusions in these two poems are pleas for a miracle rather than expectations of one.

These early poems, 'The Storme' and 'The Calme', have a power and a seriousness which match Donne's later religious poetry. Their attitude to sea-going is fiercely anti-romantic, and they share this attitude with a number of other early poems. These earlier poems are more questioning about the objectives of voyaging, more searching in their use of the image of the voyage, than the later writings are. Some of Donne's finest religious poems depend on their voyage-

imagery. How far do the valuations of the earlier poems enter
into and affect our reading of the later poems? I believe our
understanding of these later poems is deeper and richer if they
are seen to hold in themselves the memory of those earlier
valuations of the voyage and the image of the voyage.

> In what torne ship soever I embarke,
> That ship shall be my embleme of thy Arke;
> What sea soever swallow mee, that flood
> Shall be to mee an embleme of thy blood;
> Though thou with clouds of anger do disguise
> Thy face; yet through that maske I know those eyes,
>   Which, though they turne away sometimes,
>   They never will despise.

The occasion of 'A Hymne to Christ, at the Authors last going
into Germany' was Donne's appointment as chaplain to
accompany Viscount Doncaster on his embassy to Germany
in 1619; there is also a valedictory sermon preached at
Lincoln's Inn. The tone of the poem is very sombre, occupied
with the thought, even the expectation, of approaching death.
He had written to the Countess of Montgomery, 'I am going
out of the Kingdom, and perchance out of the world'.[23]

> To see God only, I goe out of sight:
>   And to scape stormy dayes, I chuse
>   An Everlasting night.

John Carey has given a reductive account of this poem,
founded on scorn for the poet for not telling the literal truth
about the short sea-journey of this well-equipped expedition.
Donne is 'enjoying a mock death'. 'His doom-laden leave-
takings acquire a theatrical appearance.' 'He takes upon
himself the glamour of martyrdom.'[24] But the poem is not a

---

23 *Selected Prose*, ed. H. Gardner and T. Healy, Oxford, Clarendon
Press, 1969, p. 151.
24 Carey, pp. 202–04.

journal or a postcard home. The prospect of a sea-journey to a foreign country has generated a poem of renunciation and dedication; separation from his friends and suspension of his normal activities are transmuted into a departure from a whole way of life. His new life, dedicated to God, will be lived in expectation of death. As in 'The Storme' and 'The Calme', the symbolic potential of the voyage dims and dwarfs the voyage itself. His new activities in Germany are not present in the picture at all. This is a great poem of commitment, and it transcends any failure there may have been in Donne to live out what here he wrote.

'In what torne ship soever I embarke.' Even if the ship were so rotten that it foundered, and he drowned, God could still be in that ship with him, and, through Christ's blood, he could attain salvation. As God would not disdain a dilapidated ship, the poet will not disdain it as an image of the ark. In earlier poems, this torn ship was a prison, or a coffin, or a cart for execution. Those other valuations are legitimate; but the poet is free to reject them here. All experiential life is a torn ship, and every ship is a prison; but if God is not in it he is not anywhere.

The sea which in the first stanza is a symbol of death, and also of Christ's blood, is in the second stanza a symbol of separation.

> I sacrifice this Iland unto thee,
> And all whom I lov'd there, and who lov'd mee;
> When I have put our seas twixt them and mee,
> Put thou thy sea betwixt my sinnes and thee.

It seems to me very important that one should see 'A Hymne to Christ' as a poem about living on a new plane, living in eager readiness for death, rather than (as commentators assume) a poem about dying. For one thing, these images of separation, from his former life, from his sins, are much weaker if they are not seen as a commitment to new standards of living. 'To see God only, I go out of sight.' Literally, he goes out of his friends' sight as the ship drops below the horizon. Figuratively, he goes out of their sight as he devotes himself wholly to God's service.

> And to scape stormy dayes, I chuse
> An Everlasting night.

Commentators are sure that Donne is here talking about death, and, of course, they are puzzled that the radiance of Heaven should be represented by night. But the collocation of stormy days and darkness recalls the horror of 'The Storme'. 'When I wakt, I saw, that I saw not.' The conclusion of the present poem contradicts the earlier one. The darkness of the storm formerly spoke of God's absence; now it speaks of His presence. Death and eternity are obviously in the poet's mind, but the force of choosing night lies in its acceptance of God's presence in the mortal gloom, as He is present in the torn ship.[25] In his use of both the torn ship and the darkness of the storm, Donne asserts his freedom to re-negotiate the currency of his images. Neither 'The Storme' nor 'A Hymne to Christ' is in the least weakened by what might appear to be oppositions in what sea-images may signify. They are wrought out of those oppositions.

* * * * *

Four years later, Donne wrote 'Hymne to God my God, in my sicknesse' (set out at the head of this chapter). Foreseeing his death, he tells us in the first stanza that he is writing the poem as a prelude to his acceptance into heaven. He will join the heavenly king's band of musicians.

> I shall be made thy Musique; As I come
> I tune the Instrument here at the dore,
> And what I must doe then, thinke now before.

25 There is an important discussion of the phrase 'Everlasting night' in *The Times Literary Supplement*, 23 December 1994, p. 6, by Geoffrey Hill, who would I think not accept this solution of what he says contemporaries would regard as 'a shocking spiritual oxymoron'.

The word 'thinke' is important in the poem: crucial indeed; it re-occurs in the fifth stanza. In heaven he will know instinctively what to play; now he can only use his imagination, improvise as best he can, guess at what he will later know.[26]

> Whilst my Physitians by their love are growne
>   Cosmographers, and I their Mapp, who lie
> Flat on this bed, that by them may be showne
>   That this is my South-west discoverie
>   *Per fretum febris*, by these streights to die,
>
> I joy, that in these straits, I see my West;
>   For, though theire currants yeeld returne to none,
> What shall my West hurt me? As West and East
>   In all flatt Maps (and I am one) are one,
>   So death doth touch the Resurrection.

Donne is a map being pored over by the cosmographer-physicians, who make out that their patient, who with dream-like swiftness is transformed from a map into a navigator, is going through the straits of suffering to reach the west of death. But their findings are a joy to him, because . . . and here there is a major stumbling-block. On a number of different occasions, in letter and sermon, Donne made the point that on a 'flat map' of the world, east and west are separated by the whole spread of the map, 'as far asunder as two points can be put'; but 'if a flat Map be but pasted upon a round Globe, the farthest East, and the farthest West meet, and are all one'.[27] The letter I have just quoted was written in the same year as the 'Hymne to God my God', in which Donne says clearly that in flat maps east and west coincide, which is not the case. Why is there this seeming mistake?

---

26 For 'think', implying imaginative supposition, see especially the series of commands in *The Second Anniversary*, 90–112. And, for mistaken supposition, 'Loves Progress' (Elegy XVIII), 54.

27 Letter to Sir Robert Ker, 1623; *Selected Prose*, p. 155. Cf. Sermons, ii, 199 and vi, 59.

In 'Upon the Annunciation and Passion falling upon one day. 1608', there is a similar assertion.

> this day hath showne,
> Th'Abridgement of Christs story, which makes one
> (As in plaine Maps, the furthest West is East)
> Of the Angels *Ave*, and *Consummatum est*.

('Plaine maps' are flat maps, maps '*in plano*', as Donne put it elsewhere.) Clearly, there is an ellipsis here. This day, marking both the annunciation of Christ's birth and the crucifixion, brings together the whole of Christ's life, making one occasion out of two widely separated events—just as west and east, though widely separated on a flat map, will come together on a round globe, or on the earth's surface. 'As in plain maps, what seems the furthest west is in fact also the furthest east' is about the shortest way to put the full argument. But there is no great difficulty about the compressed statement, not the sort of difficulty, anyway, that we experience in the 'Hymne to God my God'.

The difference seems to be in the weight given to the analogy of the map. In the annunciation poem, the analogy is no more than a parenthetical illustration of the way separated things coincide. But in the Hymn we are near to proof by analogy. The poet-patient is living within the figurative dimension of the voyage. He is travelling to the west, but he joys, because in flat maps west is east: and that demonstrates that to die is to rise with Christ. 'So death doth touch the Resurrection.' The triumphant logic of the 'as' and 'so' is similar to that in 'Aire and Angels'.

> Then as an Angell, face, and wings
> Of aire, not pure as it, yet pure doth weare,
> So thy love may be my loves spheare.

In both passages there is too much assurance about the power of a dubious analogy. In the Hymn, we might have expected a move forward from an image of the flat map, in which west and east are separated, to a globe, or the world's surface, where west and east will be seen to coincide. And *then* the triumph. As it is, the flat map unsettles the proof even as it makes it.

By collapsing the space between flat map and globe, Donne jeopardizes the entire navigational image. The flexibility of symbols of voyaging and the sea, by means of which a symbol can carry diametrically opposed meanings, in the end drains them of their power. Writing impetuously or impatiently, Donne has condensed what a flat map and a spherical map distinctively tell him. And the reason for this may be that they are equally treacherous: neither of them can truly tell him that he will rise again with Christ. This is not a question of the inadequacy of maps and 'cosmography';[28] the hollowness of deriving an assurance of immortality from a map extends to an assurance derived from imagining that you are voyaging through the seas. All arguments about his spiritual state based on analogies and metaphors from maps and navigation are brought into doubt by the dubious evidence of a flat map. 'None of thy *Indications* are *frivolous*.' The converse might be true: they all are.

The uncertainty about using a flat map to prove that 'death doth touch the Resurrection' gives tremendous force to the question which opens the following stanza.

> Is the Pacifique Sea my home? Or are
> The Easterne riches? Is *Jerusalem*?
> *Anyan*, and *Magellan*, and *Gibraltare*,
>   All streights, and none but streights, are wayes to them,
>   Whether where *Japhet* dwelt, or *Cham*, or *Sem*.

'Is the Pacifique Sea my home?' The image of home for Heaven stands firm, and makes all the stronger the question

---

28 As argued in the excellent account of the poem by Clay Hunt in *Donne's Poetry*, 1954, pp. 100–02.

whether the vast ocean is a proper symbol for his eternal dwelling. Is it any better then to use the image of eastern riches? We have already seen how they have been compromised. This stanza is about poetic images and their religious value. Donne turns back to a much older geographical symbol, Jerusalem; and again there is a question mark. The questioning is not so much resolved as given up. Whatever geographical image one uses for heaven, the way to heaven is through the pain of dying. 'None but streights, are wayes to them.'[29]

Hesitancy about our suppositions and the geographical 'proofs' that we provide for them is evident in the 'thinke' that opens the fifth stanza.

> We thinke that *Paradise* and *Calvarie*,
>   *Christs* Crosse, and *Adams* tree, stood in one place.

Helen Gardner noted that there is no authority for this idea of the identity of the two places, though there had long been a popular idea that they were in the same region.[30] This much more hesitant geographical coincidence introduces not a proof but a plea, that the sweat of his fever (the first Adam's sweat) may become the blood of Christ. I do not think it is generally noticed that there is a further all-important, but concealed, voyage-image in the poem, at the end of the fifth and the beginning of the sixth stanza. Asking that the blood of the last Adam, Christ, should embrace his soul, he continues, 'So, in his purple wrapp'd receive mee Lord'. Purple blood is also a purple gown. These lines contain the idea of death as drowning in the sea of Christ's blood which was present in the Germany Hymn. The importance of this idea for Donne may

29 John Gillies finds it striking that Donne should appear to be using a world-map, with its fictional straits of Anian, which he knew to be 'conspicuously outdated' (Gillies, p. 184). But the existence of the straits was not disproved until long after Donne's death.

30 *Divine Poems*, pp. 135–37.

be judged by what he wrote in a letter to Sir Henry Goodyer, possibly in 1608.[31]

> I would not that death should take me asleep. I would not have him meerly seise me, and onely declare me to be dead, but win me, and overcome me. When I must shipwrack, I would do it in a Sea, where mine impotencie might have some excuse; not in a sullen weedy lake, where I could not have so much as exercise for my swimming.

The consonance of this with the great 'Batter my heart' sonnet is obvious. The desire to be overwhelmed by death, as though it were to drown in a wild sea—and that sea to be Christ's blood—is very similar to the plea to God to enthral and ravish him. There is a confidence in the value of *this* image of the sea which contrasts greatly with the preceding uncertainties. Yet it is notable that so far as his soul is concerned, the poem ends not in confidence but in humble prayer to God, speaking of Christ's sacrifice, 'that he may raise the Lord throws down'.

The poem reaches a peak with the argument from a map that he will enjoy eternal life. There is a sudden descent into questioning the value of these geographical and navigational analogies, a retreat to the sea of Christ's blood and the prayer that he may be admitted to the salvation it offers.

Yet the quietness of this retreat does not appear in that other poem from this same period of illness, 'A Hymne to God the Father'. There are two versions of this noble poem but the lines in the final stanza which we particularly want are invariant.

> Wilt thou forgive that sinne where I begunne,
>   Which is my sin, though it were done before?
> Wilt thou forgive those sinnes through which I runne,
>   And doe them still: though still I doe deplore?

31 *Selected Prose*, p. 129.

> When thou hast done, thou hast not done,
>   For, I have more.

> Wilt thou forgive that sinne by which I wonne
>   Others to sinne? and, made that sinne their doore?
> Wilt thou forgive that sinne which I did shunne
>   A yeare, or two: but wallowed in, a score?
>   When thou hast done, thou hast not done,
>   For, I have more.

> I have a sinne of feare, that when I have spunne
>   My last thred, I shall perish on the shore;
> Sweare by thy selfe, that at my death thy Sunne
>   Shall shine as it shines now, and heretofore;
>   And, having done that, Thou hast done,
>   I have no more.

Balancing Donne's plea that he should die as though drowning in a sea of Christ's blood is this 'sin of fear' of a wholly different death. The sea is now an enemy; he is ship-wrecked, cast out and abandoned, dying on a foreign strand. Whether Donne knew the poem or not, it brings back sharply to mind Sir Walter Ralegh's image from his 'Ocean to Cynthia':

> So my forsaken hart, my withered mind,
> Widdow of all the joyes it once possest,
> My hopes clean out of sight, with forced wind
> To kyngdomes strange, to landes farr off addrest,

> Alone, forsaken, frindless onn the shore
> With many wounds, with deaths cold pangs inebrased,
> Writes in the dust as onn that could no more
> Whom love, and tyme, and fortune had defaced . . .[32]

Brief and uncomplicated though Donne's image is, it is powerful and compelling. Though the poem ends with the

---

32 *The Poems of Sir Walter Ralegh*, ed. A. M. C. Latham, London: Routledge and Kegan Paul, 1951, p. 28.

plea to God to save him and take him to Himself, all that voyage imagery can afford him in this poem is the bleakness of perdition.

Even if we could ascertain it, it would not matter in what order Donne wrote these two poems of his illness, and the *Devotions*. His mind was a ferment of images, and a ferment of doubt and hope about death and the future of his soul, and there is no progress to be charted. When we are asked about Donne's 'attitude to love', most of us would say that he had a dozen attitudes to love, that none of them is privileged to be 'his' beyond contradiction, and that the force of any single attitude is greatly increased by our recollection that what it professes has been contradicted in the preceding poem and will be contradicted in a different manner in the next. It is the same with voyage imagery. The metaphorical language of the sea is surrounded by a hurly-burly of signification in Donne's writing. But if there is contradiction and confusion it is constructive. Voyages of discovery become a poetics of discovery, of self-discovery. The amplitude of the varying uses and valuations in the images of voyage enriches the individual use. Attention to an image of life as a voyage is the keener when the validity of using such an image has been questioned. Above all, the range of attitudes about the riches of the far-off world, and the ethics of acquiring them by trade or conquest, is poetically invigorating because it increases tension and expands meaning. Disapproval and depreciation enter uninvited from other poems into celebrations of sexual triumph. Do they also enter into celebrations of spiritual triumph? Of course they do, but they do not cancel them out.

> Is the Pacifique Sea my home? Or are
> The Easterne riches?

They are, and they are not.

> I have a sinne of feare, that when I have spunne
> My last thred, I shall perish on the shore.

The great value of the voyage images in Donne is that in their volatility, and their free accommodation of contrasting significations, they become the means by which the play of possibilities in answering every question of importance is opened out.

PART TWO

CHAPTER FOUR—SHAKESPEARE (I): *OTHELLO*
'Verie Sea-marke of my utmost Saile'

Heere is my journies end, heere is my butt
And verie Sea-marke of my utmost Saile.

These are very familiar lines, but they have not provoked
much discussion. They seem to me to mark a vital moment in
Othello, a moment of recognition and reversal. I wish to show
in this chapter how a single metaphor can illuminate an entire
play.

Othello speaks these words in the last scene of the play. The
bodies of Desdemona and Emilia lie on the bed. Othello has
only just realized that he has been duped by Iago; he has
attacked him with his sword and been disarmed. Iago rushes
off stage pursued by Montano. Gratiano is stationed outside
to stop Othello leaving, with orders to kill him if he tries.
Othello picks up another weapon, 'a Sword of Spaine, the Ice
brookes temper'.

> *Gratiano.* What is the matter?
> *Othello.*   Behold, I have a weapon;
> A better never did it selfe sustaine
> Upon a Soldier's Thigh. I have seene the day
> That with this little Arme, and this good Sword,
> I have made my way through more impediments
> Than twenty times your stop. But (oh vain boast)
> Who can controll his Fate? 'Tis not so now.
> Be not affraid, though you do see me weapon'd;
> Heere is my journies end, heere is my butt
> And verie Sea-marke of my utmost Saile.
> Do you go backe dismaid? 'Tis a lost feare:
> Man but a Rush against *Othello's* brest,

And he retires. Where should *Othello* go?
Now: how dost thou looke now? O ill-Starr'd wench,
Pale as thy Smocke: when we shall meete at compt,
This looke of thine will hurle my Soule from Heaven,
And Fiends will snatch at it. Cold, cold, my Girle?
Even like thy Chastity. O cursed, cursed Slave!
Whip me ye Divels,
From the possession of this Heavenly sight:
Blow me about in windes, roast me in Sulphure,
Wash me in steepe-downe gulfes of Liquid fire.
O *Desdemon*! dead *Desdemon*: dead. Oh, oh!

(5. 2. 259–81)

The couplet we are considering concludes the play's extensive symbolism of the sea, and it also concludes Othello's
wandering formulations concerning the control of his own
life. It appears only in the Folio version of the play. It is a
strange thing that there should be a fundamental difference as
regards these two related matters, sea-symbolism and control
of life, between the two texts of *Othello,* the Quarto and the
Folio. In my judgement, the fuller readings of the Folio are
infinitely superior; are in fact *necessary.* While not disputing
that the Folio text may well contain Shakespeare's own
revisions, most of the Quarto's omissions and variant readings
in the areas relevant to this study look to me much more like
deterioration of the text than Shakespeare's first thoughts.
Admittedly, a brilliant revision can alter meaning and look as
though it has been there all the time; but what the Quarto
omits are essential components of the structure of extensive
passages which, taken together, form a continuous thread of
significance vital to the play. The notion that Shakespeare
stuck them in one by one at some later date and so muddled
through to his meaning is more than I can credit.

'Heere is my journies end.' To begin with, all that Othello is
saying in this couplet is, simply, 'This is where I end'. We
remember that journeys end in lovers meeting, and perhaps

Othello thinks back to the end of the journey to Cyprus. There is certainly a pause here, as the implications of his own image of life's journey develop. A journey has an end; in the sense of a termination. It also has an end in the sense of an objective or purpose; a place it is directed towards. So he goes on to say, not 'To this I have been brought', but 'To this point I have steered. This is the destination I have been working for.' The couplet, spoken with intense bitterness, is the revelation to himself of the futility of his every aspiration.

A butt is a goal; literally, a target; as in *Henry V*, 1. 2. 186: 'To which is fixed as an ayme or butt, / Obedience . . .' Sea-mark is a potent image. Literally any prominent object which could act as a guide for seamen—tower or steeple or promontory—it was used by Shakespeare to indicate something invulnerable, indifferent to the violence of storms, a guiding-point or objective that gives direction and meaning to one's life. In *Coriolanus*, the hero wishes that his son may prove—

> To shame unvulnerable, and sticke i' th Warres
> Like a great Sea-marke standing every flaw,
> And saving those that eye thee. (5. 3. 73–75)

In Sonnet 116, love is 'an ever fixed marke / That lookes on tempests and is never shaken', and, in a corresponding image, it is 'the star to every wandring barke'.

That a man apprehended for the murder of his wife, on what he now realizes to be totally false evidence of her infidelity, should describe his situation as an arrival at a long-sought destination is very surprising and very alarming. And it is the sense of finality, of completion, that is so impressive: the 'very sea-mark of my utmost sail'. It seems to me that this couplet is the fullest admission of personal responsibility made by any of Shakespeare's tragic heroes. All the actions of his life have been leading him towards this final act, the murder of the innocent Desdemona.

A moment or two before, Othello was going to fight his way out of the chamber. To do what? Presumably to exact retribution by killing Iago; certainly to free himself from bondage and do *something*. It is almost a matter of instinct with him to fight his way out of a perilous situation; and his present predicament is easier to escape from than many earlier ones. But to say that he can easily fight his way out of such tight corners now seems to him merely a vain boast. Formerly these 'haire-breadth scapes i' th' imminent deadly breach' (1. 3. 136) were his pride. He won Desdemona by describing them. They are now emptied of value. 'Who can controll his Fate?' The words 'oh vain boast' apply equally to fighting your way out and to controlling your fate. To fight your way out is to attempt to control your fate.

With ''Tis not so now', Othello is not saying that this occasion is different from all the others; that at *this* juncture he is unable to control his fate. He is looking at the past as well as the present. He means that it is not possible now, any more than it was in the past, to control your fate by acts of desperate courage.

He tells Gratiano not to fear any act of his; he has done with all action. 'Heere is my journies end . . .' In any case, 'Where should *Othello* go?' In two of its applications this receives the answer that there is nowhere to go. There is nowhere to go because all previous purposeful action has led only to this point; activity is counterproductive, a weapon that recoils upon its user. Secondly, it is not conceivable to him that history, so far as he is concerned, should extend beyond this point; it has absolute finality, 'my utmost Saile'; he has no future. In another application, however, there is a very different answer. There is no way forward in mortal life. But by killing Desdemona he has damned himself. He has already placed himself in a state of being in which his physical movements can be of no help to him whatever. He was aware, before he knew he had been duped, that, if he had acted without just cause, 'I were damn'd beneath all depth in hell' (line 137).

The future tense of 'when we shall meete at compt' collapses into the present. 'O cursed, cursed Slave!' He *is* accursed. The repetition of the word in the Folio is absolutely right; the Quarto has simply 'O cursed slave'. Right also is the almost immediate use by Lodovico of the same phrase for Iago (line 292). Many editions prefer the Quarto's 'damned slave', but the identification of the two men is important.

Now follows the most discussed part of the speech, the impassioned exclamation, 'Whip me ye divels . . .' and so on. The seeming extravagance of Othello's outburst alienates many. Modern editions add considerably to the appearance of frenzy by studding the speech with exclamation marks, and suggesting repeated piercing cries by reproducing the 'Oh, oh!' of the Folio or the 'O, o, o' of the Quarto, disregarding the fact that such repetitions were the conventional represent-ation of an extended groan—as in the dying moments of both Hamlet and Lear. F. R. Leavis regarded Othello's words at this point as 'an intolerably intensified form of the common 'I could kick myself'.[1] But the words are perhaps not intolerably intensified if they are regarded as Othello's recognition that he is eternally damned and eternally separated from Desdemona. His outburst begins with naming himself accursed, and ends with the repeated statement that Desdemona is dead. He is accepting the horrors and torments of hell and inviting the devil to begin the suffering which he has incurred because Desdemona is dead, by his hand. It is strange though that a moment later he says, 'in my sense 'tis happinesse to die' (line 290). It is an obvious, perhaps too obvious, link, with what he said when reunited with Desdemona after the storm: 'If it were now to dye, / 'Twere now to be most happy'. Then he would have been happy to die because he was with Des-demona; now it would be happiness to die because he has lost Desdemona. But he seems oddly indifferent to the pains of hell.

There *is* one further action remaining to him; to set the seal

1 Leavis, p. 150.

on his acknowledgement that he is damned by committing suicide. His act of stabbing himself he defines by analogy as a service to the Venetian state, by ridding it of one of its enemies; perhaps he considers it also a higher service: an acceptance of his eternal sentence.

*   *   *   *   *

Having begun at the end of the play, I want to go back to the beginning to explore what Othello could have meant by his extraordinary remark that the deathbed of Desdemona was the 'verie Sea-marke of my utmost Saile'; not merely the conclusion of his life, but the beacon he had directed himself towards.

Much is made in the first act of *Othello* of choosing a course of life and committing oneself to it. Desdemona says:

> That I did love the Moore, to live with him,
> My downe-right violence, and storme of Fortunes,
> May trumpet to the world. My heart's subdu'd
> Even to the very quality of my Lord. (1. 3. 248–45)[2]

Later in the same scene, Iago, who vows to serve himself, not others, and to exercise his malevolence on both Othello and Cassio, tells Roderigo that our future is in our own power. ''Tis in our selves that we are thus, or thus. Our Bodies are our Gardens, to the which our Wills are Gardiners.' And he believes of course that he can choose a future not only for himself but for others.

Othello's commitment is cautious. He tells Iago that he is not afraid of any procedures that might be taken against him for having married Desdemona. His services to the state will outweigh complaints against him; his ancestry is royal; his merits measure up to the distinction of his marriage.

---

2 The word 'did' is supplied from the Quarto, which instead of 'very quality' has the unfortunate 'utmost pleasure'.

> For know *Iago*,
> But that I love the gentle *Desdemona*,
> I would not my unhoused free condition
> Put into Circumscription, and Confine,
> For the Seas worth. (1. 2. 24–28)

It is a curious conclusion. Having defined his personal
position as unassailable in terms of his service to the state, the
nobility of his descent, and his own merits, he feels impelled to
answer an unspoken question: 'Why, then, have you compromised this position by getting married?' It is clear that the
circumscription and confine into which he feels he has entered
is not alone the jeopardy of social antagonism, but the quality
of married life. The description of his previous life as
'unhoused' shows that. In spite of having remarked on a life of
service, Othello sees himself surrendering freedom and
accepting limitation. The dedication to love is an infringement
of his being, but the heavy price—valued at the sea's worth—is
worth paying.

Othello's conception of his unmarried self as autonomous,
free, owing nothing to others, has to be carried into the
description of his past life in the following scene—telling the
Senate what he had told Desdemona. It was the story of a
soldier he had related, of the perils of battle and siege.

> I spoke of most disastrous chances:
> Of moving Accidents by Flood and Field,
> Of haire-breadth scapes i' th' imminent deadly breach,
> Of being taken by the Insolent Foe,
> And sold to slavery. Of my redemption thence,
> And portance in my Travellours historie.

In this last line there is one of these critical textual differences.
In the Quarto it reads, 'And with it all my travells Historie'.
Some editions which give the Folio's 'portance' jib at 'travel-
ler's history', but, as Greenblatt remarked,[3] the Folio seems to

3 Greenblatt, p. 237.

be 'noting the genre'. Othello was not a traveller but a soldier, but what he had to relate about cannibals and anthopophagi and vast caves and barren deserts made his story seem like a traveller's tale. His tone is the amused (and perilous) understatement of the speech's conclusion:

> She lov'd me for the dangers I had past,
> And I lov'd her, that she did pity them.
> This onely is the witch-craft I have us'd.

But the chief inadequacy of the Quarto here is the omission of 'portance'. The whole line means, 'How I conducted, or comported myself during these strange vicissitudes'.

The Quarto reading, 'my travells Historie', might seem to have some justification in Othello referring to his earlier life as a 'Pilgrimage' (line 153). It is an important question in the context of this study whether Othello means that he thought of his life as heading somewhere, or whether the word pilgrimage is used fairly casually, as it could be, for journeying through life. Is he speaking of wandering or of purposeful self-direction? More often than not in Shakespeare the words pilgrim/pilgrimage have the sense of mission towards a desired goal. Essentially, however, Othello's narrative is not a story of free movement towards an objective, but a story of the service of a soldier reacting to circumstances. He does not speak of his aims, of how he moulded his life, but of how he conducted himself in the situations which because of his profession he found himself in; how he survived the dangers, how he came out of these situations—with honour.

One has to supply the word 'honour' from the final scene, when Othello, finding himself disarmed, swallows the disgrace: 'Why should Honor out-live Honesty?' (line 245) (William Empson rightly said that this question 'sums up the play',[4] and we shall return to it). As we have seen, he has viewed himself in this ultimate encounter as repeating one of

4 Empson (1951), p. 228.

those earlier feats of fighting his way out of danger. To attain or preserve honour must always have been the controlling factor, the goal that made his life a pilgrimage. He does not speak, as Iago does, of the purposeful planning of his future. Later in the play he talks of 'the bigge Warres, / That makes Ambition, Vertue' (3. 3. 349–50). He was a professional soldier and by his skill and courage he won the advancement he looked for. But that is not the same as long-term planning. His aim in life was to acquit himself with honour in adverse circumstances.

The structure of *Othello* is that of a figure-of-eight on its side. Othello and Desdemona are united in Venice at the start, then separated by the storm on their voyage to Cyprus. Reunited at Cyprus they are separated again by Iago's scheming, then at the end they are together again, though not united, in death. The storm at sea balances the storm raised by Iago.[5] Shakespeare put the storm into the story. In the source, Giraldi says of the Moor and his lady that they set off 'and with a sea of the utmost tranquillity arrived safely in Cyprus'.[6] Shakespeare makes the tempest as violent as possible, and contrasts the safe arrival and joyous reunion of bride and bridegroom in the haven at Cyprus with the 'journey's end' of the planned death in the bedchamber.

As Iago's insinuations begin to unsettle Othello, the course of his life is offered to us in contradictory images. First, he grandly shuffles off responsibility for what he mistakenly thinks has happened on to 'destiny unshunnable' (3. 3. 275). Cuckoldry is 'the plague to great ones':

> Even then, this forked plague is Fated to us
> When we do quicken.

By becoming great, Othello has entered a group who are doomed from birth! That the notion of making a free and

5 Cf. Knight, p. 111.
6 Bullough, vol. 7, 1973, p. 243.

considered choice in marrying Desdemona has been overtaken by a notion of a predestined lot is confirmed by his extraordinary remark in the speech about the handkerchief (3. 4. 63–65). His mother gave it to him when she was dying, he said, 'And bid me (when my Fate would have me Wiv'd) / To give it her'. How *necessary* the passive voice of the Folio ('Wiv'd') is, compared with the Quarto's active 'would have me wive'!

The convenient notion that he is subject to fate is dramatically contradicted by the image of total personal control in the 'Pontic Sea' speech. (The whole speech is absent in the Quarto.) Othello summons 'blacke vengeance' and demands blood. He assures Iago that his mind will not change.

> Never *Iago*. Like to the Ponticke Sea,
> Whose Icie Current, and compulsive course,
> Nev'r [knows] retyring ebbe, but keeps due on
> To the Proponticke, and the Hellespont:
> Even so my bloody thoughts, with violent pace
> Shall nev'r looke backe, nev'r ebbe to humble Love,
> Till that a capeable, and wide Revenge
> Swallow them up. (3. 3. 453–60)

Othello becomes the sea, the all-powerful controller, creating destiny unshunnable. It is in this spirit that he enters the bedchamber in Act 5, scene 2, the loving executioner, Justice itself (line 17), to carry out his death sentence on Desdemona.

But, as we have seen, when he has killed her and then learned that he has been duped, he demotes his identity from the sea itself to that of a voyager by sea, who has steered his ship to this appalling conclusion.

Othello regarded his life as a pilgrimage of honour. To the service of the state he added the service of Desdemona, understanding that thereby he had limited his freedom and unalterably changed the nature of his life.

> There, where I have garnerd up my heart,
> Where either I must live, or beare no life;
> The Fountaine from the which my currant runnes,
> Or else dries up. (4.2. 57–60)

After the brief period of fulfilment and happiness, his uncertainly about a commitment which was curiously hedged about to begin with is everywhere apparent. 'Why did I marry?' Saddling fate rather than his own free choice with responsibility for his condition, he laments the loss of his true life by his change of status. He cannot go back to being just a soldier—but this is the life he laments the loss of when he thinks his wife unfaithful. He bids farewell to 'the Pride, Pompe, and Circumstance of glorious Warre'; 'Farewell: *Othello's* Occupation's gone' (3. 3. 345–57). Exchanging the service of Desdemona for the service of Iago, he asserts in the strongest possible form the freedom to act which he had formerly claimed as belonging to his unmarried status, and pledges himself to an act of honour to expunge his wife's dishonour.

At the centre of Othello's 'recognition' in the sea-mark couplet, and his assumption of total responsibility for what has happened, is his understanding that he has been driven by what he now understands to be a corrupted code of honour. 'Why should Honor out-live Honesty?', he asked. 'Let it go all.' Honesty has been hi-jacked by the discredited Iago whom Othello had thought the most honest of people. It Othello believes that his conception of honesty was all wrong, and that he himself has been grossly dishonest, then it follows, not so much that he has no claim to honour, as that his conception of honour has become untenable. Empson had an excellent paragraph on the unbreakable connection between 'honour' and 'honesty' in the play: 'a test of one is a test of the other'.[7]

The force of Othello's repudiation of a false idea of honour comes in his *not* attempting to break out of the chamber with

7 Empson (1951), p. 229.

his 'Sword of Spaine'. It was a question of repeating one of
those dare-devil escapes of his youth. It is now vain to boast of
such triumphs; the presumption is that they are seen to be
misguided not only because they were fruitless attempts to
control fate, but because what motivated them was a code of
honour which has led him astray. The repudiation may be seen
in his answer to Lodovico's question as he enters: 'Where is
this rash, and most unfortunate man?' 'That's he that was
Othello: heere I am' (line 284).

Those critics, so many of them, who see Othello in the final
scene as wallowing in self-pity, self-exculpation and self-
dramatization, do not perceive the self-laceration of his ironic
reply to Lodovico's further question, 'What shall be saide to
thee?'

> Why any thing;
> An honourable Murderer, if you will;
> For nought I did in hate, but all in Honour.

So far from trying to palliate his crime, he blackens it with the
oxymoron. He killed Desdemona by following the code
which had governed him all his life. Jane Adamson writes:
'The bravado and the self-justification are preposterous'.[8] It is
extraordinary to describe Othello's self-contempt in this way.
Some years earlier than this remark was made, Bernard
McElroy had written: 'This is grim paradox, not shallow self-
justification . . . The Moor's reply is bitter self-mockery'.[9]
Othello is not justifying himself; for him, the most horrible
thing about this crime is that he carried it out with the best
intentions. It is his code of honour that has led him to commit
murder. 'Why should Honor out-live Honesty? Let it go all.'

The reason that most accounts of Othello's feelings in the
last scene go awry is that they do not give him credit for the
grim, sardonic, bitter humour with which he describes

8 Adamson, p. 292.
9 McElroy, p. 142.

them.[10] The intense light now revealing himself to himself has a marked effect on the dry humour that has always been there: 'Keepe up your bright Swords, for the dew will rust them'. Or, 'This onely is the witch-craft I have us'd'. It is a good actor who makes Othello smile when he says:

If after every Tempest, come such Calmes,
May the windes blow, till they have waken'd death!

This humour acidifies in the aftermath of the murder. The chamber of death is 'verie Sea-marke of my utmost Saile'. He speaks those words in the same tone that he tells Lodovico that, if he likes, he can call him an honourable murderer; and the acerbic self-mockery continues into his picture of himself as 'one that lov'd not wisely, but too well', as McElroy noted. Othello has been a fool of the first order, as he himself recognizes. 'O Foole, foole, foole!' But he is not in this last scene the simpleton whom critics make him out to be, proffering absurd excuses for his action. Each 'excuse' is a further self-condemnation by a man who is not in the business of making light of a crime which he believes has brought him to eternal damnation.

And yet, 'who can controll his Fate?' At the same time that he accepts responsibility and accepts the punishment for his crime, Othello knows that though his actions have brought about the catastrophe, he has not directed the course of events. As with every sea-voyager under sail, where you get to depends as much on the elements as on your own navigation.

'My Boate sailes freely, both with winde and Streame' (2. 3. 63). It was Iago who directed the course of events, however much Othello was responsible for his own actions. In their final meeting, Othello addresses the bystanders.

10 R. B. Heilman hesitated for a moment: 'It is possible that combining "honourable" with "murderer" may be a bitter irony at his own expense'. But, having faith in 'Othello's general incapacity for the oblique', he rejected the possibility (Heilman, p. 164).

> Will you, I pray, demand that demy-Divell,
> Why he hath thus ensnar'd my Soule and Body?

Iago refuses to speak, and, not surprisingly, Othello com-
mends his silence. 'Well, thou dost best.' What kind of useful
answer could Iago conceivably give?

It is no more possible to understand *Othello* than it is to
understand *Hamlet* unless it is seen as fundamentally a
religious play.[11] Both heroes tread a narrow and perilous path
that they believe to be right while fearing it may be damnable.
Othello is saturated with reference to damnation.[12] The two
plays are quite different, but in both the mystery of the
interplay between personal choice and supernatural pressure,
both divine and demonic, in bringing the conclusion about, is
where the interest finally lies. The problem is utterly unreal
for us, and that's why we have such trouble understanding
Shakespearian tragedy.

In the speech we have been considering, Othello has gone
far beyond admitting that he has made a terrible mistake,
through being terribly misled. Having come to a point in his
life when movement in any direction is unimaginable, the
whole of his past life looks hideously like a journey directing
itself towards his crime, a crime for which he must suffer
eternal punishment. What factors may have led him to give
such rash and speedy credit to Iago's falsehoods—his colour,
his age, his foreignness—become for the moment less important under the gaze of Othello's self-condemnation. His
attention is on a falsely directed life, a course plotted by false
navigational aids. No doubt he is too hard on himself in his
self-condemnation, but the anagnorisis is that an imperfect
understanding of his objectives throughout his life has
brought about an imperfect understanding of himself and
those he relates to, and that it is this inadequacy which has
brought him to his fatal mistrust. All along he served an idea of

11 Edwards (1986), p. 45.
12 See Bethell, *passim*.

honour which he has come to recognize as wrongly founded. His renunciation of honour looks forward to Milton's recognition that what is ordinarily called heroism belongs to a fallen world.

Othello did himself an injustice to call Desdemona's death-bed the sea-mark of his utmost sail, but the wave of revulsion concerning his life which the phrase implies is a very important element in our judgment of the final moments of Othello's life, and it seems generally overlooked. At the end of the novel, *The Silent Cry*, by Kenzaburo Oe, the narrator realizes that he cannot follow his friend and his brother into the great gesture of suicide because he does not know what truth he would cry aloud to those who went on living.

> If I hadn't yet grasped the 'truth', I was unlikely to find the strength of purpose to take that final plunge into death. It hadn't been like that with great grandfather's brother and Takahashi just before they died: they had been sure of their own hell, and in crying out the 'truth' had risen above it.[13]

13 Translation by John Bester.

CHAPTER FIVE—SHAKESPEARE (II): *MACBETH*

'And swallow Navigation up'

Though the yesty Waves
Confound and swallow Navigation up . . .
. . . Answer me
To what I aske you.

4. 1. 53–54, 60–61

Images of blood, sleep, the stage, clothes, nature, light are much more prominent in *Macbeth* than images of voyaging. But the sea is most certainly present, as in Macbeth's words above, and in his great question and answer:

Will all great *Neptunes* Ocean wash this blood
Cleane from my Hand? no: this my Hand will rather
The multitudinous Seas incarnadine,
Making the Greene one Red.

2. 2. 57–60

Images of the sea, of storm, and of voyaging in fact maintain a powerful underlying presence in *Macbeth*, having to do (as in *Othello*) with the issue of control over one's life.

We begin with the second scene. The wounded captain, giving his account of Macbeth's conduct against the rebels, describes how Macbeth slaughtered Macdonwald, then pauses before going on to tell of the Norwegian reinforcements coming to the aid of the rebels.

As whence the Sunne 'gins his reflection,
Shipwracking Stormes, and direfull Thunders [break]:
So from that Spring, whence comfort seem'd to come,
Discomfort swells.

1. 2. 25–28

The word 'break' is Pope's addition to what seems to be an imperfect line in the Folio. Most editors agree that 'whence the Sunne 'gins his reflection' refers to the vernal equinox, with 'reflection' meaning 'turning back'. This strained interpretation surely misses the whole point of the passage. No doubt editors are affected by the word 'spring', though it here means 'source'. 'Reflection' can hardly mean a turning-back in this equinoctial sense. The word means 'shining', and Shakespeare uses the word equally for direct and indirect shining. What the captain means is that from the self-same point of the compass from which you get the first heartening rays of the sun you can also get the fiercest of storms—storms that will wreck a ship. So, Macbeth's moment of triumph was suddenly transformed into a moment of extreme danger. It is a commonplace enough thought. But it seems important that it should be made at this point in the play, in this image.

Macbeth is founded on doubleness, and the merging of opposites. Things which are contrary occupy the same space, share the same appearance. Fair is foul and foul is fair. Nothing is but what is not. Goodness is forced to share its semblance with usurping evil, as Malcolm says.

> Angels are bright still, though the brightest fell.
> Though all things foule would wear the brows of grace,
> Yet Grace must still looke so.   4. 3. 22–24

So the captain's simile, describing how a moment of triumph became a moment of great danger, reinforces the duplicity and paradox which inform the play, and puts them in terms of the treachery of weather for a sea-going vessel. Like the first Thane of Cawdor, on whom Duncan 'built / An absolute Trust', so the second, Macbeth, will be both the beneficent sun and the destroying storm. The simile is also an important link between the first appearance of the weird sisters, amid thunder and lightning, which precedes the account of the rebellion and its suppression, and their second, which is all about storms and voyaging.

Thunder. Enter the three Witches.
1. Where hast thou beene, Sister?
2. Killing Swine.
3. Sister, where thou?
1. A Saylors wife had Chestnuts in her Lappe,
And mouncht, and mouncht, and mouncht. Give me,
quoth I.
Aroynt thee, Witch! the rumpe-fed Ronyon cries.
Her Husband's to Aleppo gone, Master o' th' *Tiger*:
But in a Syve Ile thither sayle,
And like a Rat without a tayle,
Ile doe, Ile doe, and Ile doe.
2. Ile give thee a Winde.
1. Th' art kinde.
3. And I another.
1. I my selfe have all the other,
And the very Ports they blow,
All the Quarters that they know
I' th' Ship-mans Card.
Ile dreyne him drie as Hay;
Sleepe shall neyther Night nor Day
Hang upon his Pent-house Lid:
He shall live a man forbid:
Wearie Sev'nights, nine times nine,
Shall he dwindle, peake, and pine:
Though his Barke cannot be lost,
Yet it shall be Tempest-tost.
Looke what I have.
2. Shew me, shew me.
1. Here I have a Pilots Thumbe,
Wrackt, as homeward he did come. *Drum within.*
3. A Drumme, a Drumme:
Macbeth doth come.

1. 3. 1–31

In a play as compressed and taut as *Macbeth*, vibrating with the sound of unacted scenes, the expansiveness of the Witch's proposed revenge on the luckless and unoffending master of the Tiger, doing nothing to forward the action, forces attention on itself. The whole scene has immense choric and thematic value, transposing so much of the human activity of the play on to another plane, altering both the perspective and the scale of values. 'Killing Swine' is a laconic and reductive analogue of the lengthy account of Macbeth's heroic slaughter of Macdonwald. The repeated 'Ile doe'—a verb without an object—anticipates the almost obsessional use of the word by Macbeth and his wife, and their continuous counterproductive activity. The control of the winds shows, in this weather-conscious play, the massive power of the weird sisters, just as their inability to wreck the sailor's ship shows its limitations.

Although in the fate proposed for the master of the *Tiger*—the sleepless torment of 'a man forbid'—there is an obvious foretaste of what is to happen to Macbeth, another victim of the witches, it is equally obvious that not the suffering of Macbeth but the suffering of *his* victims is chiefly glanced at here, especially that of Lady Macduff, persecuted because Macbeth resents her husband's actions.[1] In Macbeth's case, the witches will translate their victim into the likeness of themselves.

'Though his Barke cannot be lost.' The witch may propose to torment the master beyond endurance, but he is in the end protected by a higher power. In a passage we shall shortly be examining, Rosse says that under Macbeth's tyranny the people of Scotland are floating helplessly on a wild and violent sea. When we think about their imminent rescue by Malcolm and the English force, our minds go back to the master of the *Tiger*, tempest-tossed, though his bark cannot be lost. Macbeth's bark, on the contrary, is certainly lost, his 'eternal jewel' given to the common enemy of man. 'Blow Winde!

1 Compare Marienstras, p. 83.

come wracke!', he shouts before the final battle. He is not the master of the *Tiger*, saved in the end, but the pilot 'wrackt, as homeward he did come'. The Witch obscenely displays his severed thumb; at the end of the play Malcolm displays Macbeth's severed head. This passage about the master of the *Tiger*, standing at the head of the scene of the prophecy which generates the whole action of the play, sets up a thematic image of that action in which Macbeth is both a scion of the witches bringing storm and tempest to the people of Scotland, and also the pilot of a vessel that is wrecked.

The doubleness of *Macbeth*, in which there is the darkness of night during the day and the dead behave as if they were alive, extends also to the dimension of time, in the confusion between present and future. For Macbeth, his 'single state' is so shaken by 'horrible Imaginings', that 'Function / Is smother'd in surmise'. Lady Macbeth says that she feels 'the future in the instant'. It is the domination of the present by the image of the future, obliterating sequence, or the steps by which the future is properly to be reached, which is their undoing. The diagram of time being lost to them, as though on a chart departure-point and destination were the same, true navigation becomes impossible. But there is a further all-important element which makes their progress towards becoming king and queen of Scotland a black denial of the voyage of life.

It is evident from Lady Macbeth's crucial speeches in 1. 7, abusing Macbeth for his decision to 'proceed no further in this Businesse', that in the past the two of them have furtively enjoyed imagining themselves as king and queen, and in the security of their day-dream, have contemplated the means of attaining 'the ornament of life'; that is, doing away with the present occupant of the throne. Not only (apparently) did Macbeth 'breake this enterprize' to his wife, but he swore to carry out the murder. The secret excitement of becoming king and queen through a great sacrilegious act may have been at least as strong as the pleasure of the thought of actually reigning as king. 'Aspiration to the kingship', writes Nicholas Grene, 'is overwhelmingly an imagination of transgression'.[2] In a fine passage on Macbeth's fascination with 'the abyss of evil', J. I. M. Stewart said that 'it is veritably the crime and not the crown that compels Macbeth'.[3] At any rate, kingship and murder are indissolubly together in the minds of both Macbeth and his wife. No sooner have the witches made their prophecy to Macbeth than the 'horrid Image' of the 'suggestion' (prompting) of murder is making his heart knock at his ribs, against the use of nature. It is stranger still with Lady Macbeth. No sooner has she read her husband's letter conveying the promise of kingship than she is worrying whether Macbeth has the guts to perform the necessary murder. The prophecy seems to be not a release from the need to murder but an encouragement to it, an authorization of it, a guarantee of its successful outcome. Murder is, simply, 'the neerest way' to the crown, and she gives herself up to the mental performance of it in her voluptuous embrace of evil.

The spontaneous, almost instinctive, linking of monarchy and murder in their minds is extraordinary. Who in their right senses, if promised as an absolute certainty that they would shortly be receiving a million pounds, would go out and rob a bank to make sure of getting the money? Shakespeare lets the thought of waiting for the future just flit into Macbeth's mind, not to re-appear. 'If Chance will have me King, / Why Chance may Crowne me, / Without my stirre' (1. 3. 142–44). Imagination has erased the gap between present and future, and has replaced it with a bridge of crime, the only way to that further shore. The present, the crime, and the future are all fused together. It is a kind of rape of the future that they perform, an act of violence against the natural sequence of things imaged in Duncan's words to Macbeth himself: 'I have begun to plant thee, and will labour / To make thee full of

2 Grene, p. 198.
3 Stewart, p. 93.

growing'. The idea of being as it were in competition with time is present in his cry when Macduff escapes him: 'Time, thou anticipat'st my dread exploits'.

The horror of transposing sacrilegious murder from the realm of fantasy into that of reality is the core of the play. Macbeth's revulsion from the consequences of an actual assassination is countered by his wife's taunts about his virility and, as he takes those steps which he beseeches the earth not to hear, the image of pity in his mind, the naked new-born babe, is succeeded by that of the air-borne dagger—'a Dagger of the Minde', no less real to him. The central words in the whole magnificent complexity which Shakespeare creates are those spoken to the aerial dagger: 'Thou marshall'st me the way that I was going'. To the confusion of present and future, the confusion of the real and the imaginary, must be added the confusion in his mind about whether he is moving of his own free will and choice, or whether he is being driven by 'supernaturall solliciting' and fate. He had already chosen the path he is being drawn along.

'I goe, and it is done.' Present and future are elided, vaulting ambition o'er-leaps itself and falls on the other side. But there is the necessary physical act between 'I goe' and 'it is done'. A hardened soldier who has sliced his enemies open is stupefied by the actuality of Duncan's blood and the strength of his own conscience. He stares at his hands.

> Hah! they pluck out mine Eyes.
> Will all great *Neptunes* Ocean wash this blood
> Cleane from my Hand? no: this my Hand will rather
> The multitudinous Seas incarnadine,
> Making the Greene one Red.

2. 2. 56–60

Macbeth measures the enormity of his crime in archetypal imagery of sleep and the sea. He has murdered sleep; he will pollute the ocean. Sleep is innocence and rest. The ocean is a great cleanness. In Macbeth's view, his crime has poisoned them both; changed them as utterly as Adam's sin changed the face of nature. 'Multitudinous' is a very curious word. Shakespeare uses it in one other place only, when Coriolanus advises the senate not to provide representation for the people. 'At once plucke out / The Multitudinous Tongue.' It is a revolting image: disenfranchisement—taking away the people's voice—becomes a violent mutilation of a composite person. But it is that person, amalgamating all the individual plebeians, who helps us with the *Macbeth* passage. Editors offer suggestions that 'the multitudinous Seas' means a multitude of seas, or the seas with their multitude of creatures, and no doubt both of these meanings lie somewhere within the capacious phrase. But in the first place the turbulence of an unruly sea might well have suggested the restlessness of the 'many-headed multitude', and by this comparison of the wide ocean to a vast milling crowd, the sea is made human. Macbeth's crime—so it seems to him—has destroyed sleep and stained the lives of multitudes.

This sea in which Macbeth cannot wash himself clean becomes the sea of blood through which he visualizes himself wading in the great hinge-passage ending the scene of Banquo's spectral appearance at the feast.

> For mine owne good,
> All causes shall give way. I am in blood
> Stept in so farre, that should I wade no more,
> Returning were as tedious as go ore.
>
> 3. 4. 134–37

Though neither of these great sea-images has anything in itself to do with voyaging, the sea is the one sea, in which you wash, through which you wade, on which you sail in storm and tempest, in which you are wrecked.

Since the navigation from present to future has been preempted by confusion of every kind, it is hardly surprising that where the Macbeths find themselves is not where they thought they were going. Macbeth has won a fruitless crown and a barren sceptre. To regain control of the future, he renegotiates his identity, seeking to expunge that terrifying chasm between imagining a deed and performing it which has hitherto possessed and dominated him. But at the very time he makes his resolve to act without pausing to consider, he also decides to visit the weird sisters—to know what his future is to be. As before, he is equally sure that he chooses his own path and that it is chosen for him.   Macbeth addresses the witches.

> I conjure you, by that which you Professe,
> (How ere you come to know it) answer me:
> Though you untye the Windes, and let them fight
> Against the Churches: Though the yesty Waves
> Confound and swallow Navigation up:
> Though bladed Corne be lodg'd, and Trees blown downe,
> Though Castles topple on their Warders heads:
> Though Pallaces, and Pyramids do slope
> Their heads to their Foundations: Though the treasure
> Of Natures Germaine, tumble altogether,
> Even till destruction sicken: Answer me
> To what I aske you.
>
> 4. 1. 50–61

'Though the yesty Waves / Confound and swallow Navigation up . . .' The compilers of the *Oxford English Dictionary* thought that 'navigation' had the concrete meaning of 'shipping', although the first appearance of such a meaning apart from this is not until 1748. The *OED* meaning is supported in the Oxford edition by Nicholas Brooke—almost the only editor to think that the word needs explanation. This interpretation certainly brings the word into line with the other nouns: churches, castles and palaces; what the yesty waves will swallow is ships. But Macbeth is not really contemplating things being flattened; he is thinking about whole institutions and ways of life being destroyed—religion, agriculture, government—and then life itself. Each noun is a synecdoche for an activity essential for social life. The normal meaning of 'navigation' at this time was voyaging, moving from one place to another in a ship. If we make 'navigation' mean ships, to enable them to be sunk, we quickly have to return it to mean voyaging in order to get its full and proper signification. For when Macbeth says 'navigation' he is using the word as a metaphor for the purposeful direction of one's life.

What Macbeth is saying is bombast, perhaps; an exaggerated way of declaring that *whatever happens* he is determined to know. But he means it, too. In refusing to tread back the way that he has come, the way of contrition ('as tedious as go ore'), and placing the preservation of himself above all other considerations, he is accepting the regimen of the witches and their master, and cooperating with them in their destruction of soul and body. In listing the things he is prepared to sacrifice, he names what, in spite of his commitment, he most deeply believes in. That he should place 'navigation' so high in his list is absorbing. His own sense of self-direction, in spiritual and material terms, has been enigmatic and equivocal; he knows he is not free. But here he reveals his deep-down sense that controlling one's course of life—the freedom of the will and the responsibility of personal choice—is an ultimate value of human existence. By the end of the play, however, he has lost this bedrock conviction.

Rosse, as it were, takes up the navigation image and enforces its deep importance in the next passage we are considering, from the next scene.

> But cruell are the times, when we are Traitors
> And do not know our selves:when we hold Rumor
> From what we feare, yet know not what we feare,
> But floate upon a wilde and violent Sea
> Each way, and move. I take my leave of you . . .
> 4. 2. 18–22

The people of Scotland, I suggested, are to be seen in the condition of the master of the *Tiger*, the tempest-tossed victims of the witches. The collaborator, Macbeth, has taken the place of the Second Witch, and is denying to his subjects the power of navigation. The word 'move' has caused much concern, and many emendations have been proposed. It is essential that the Folio reading (as given here) be preserved. That they float 'each way' emphasizes their loss of direction and control. The image of material floating listlessly to and fro obviously affected Shakespeare; he included it twice in *Antony and Cleopatra*, first to compare the contrariness of public opinion with 'a Vagabond Flagge upon the Streame', going to and back with the tide, 'to rot it selfe with motion', and later to compare Octavia's divided heart with 'the Swannes downe feather / That stands upon the Swell at the full of Tide: / And neither way inclines'. Both these passages enforce the necessity of keeping the Folio reading, 'Each way, and move', because it is the issue of movement that matters. Purposeful movement, that which belongs to 'navigation', has become impossible. This helpless 'each way' drifting is the only way they are able to move; the words 'and move' mean 'and move only in this manner'. The view of some editors that Rosse breaks off his sentence with the word 'move' is not unjustified. At least he is pausing on this word, reflecting on a movement that is moving nowhere.

Having (so to speak) wrecked his own ship, Macbeth has denied 'navigation' to others. Like a shipwrecked sailor, he clings to the plank that's offered him in order to save himself: the witches' promises, and their instruction to 'be bloody, bold, and resolute'. The great 'Tomorrow' speech, which conspicuously does *not* use voyage-imagery, is all the same deeply affected by the play's subliminal voyage motif.

> *Macbeth.* . . . Wherefore was that cry?
> *Seyton* . The Queene (my Lord) is dead.
> *Macbeth* . She should have dy'de heereafter;
> There would have beene a time for such a word:
> To morrow, and to morrow, and to morrow,

Creepes in this petty pace from day to day,
To the last Syllable of Recorded time:
And all our yesterdayes, have lighted Fooles
The way to dusty death. Out, out, breefe Candle,
Life's but a walking Shadow, a poore Player,
That struts and frets his houre upon the Stage,
And then is heard no more. It is a Tale
Told by an Ideot, full of sound and fury,
Signifying nothing.

5. 5. 15–28

It is scarcely credible that with 'She should have dy'de heereafter' Macbeth meant, 'Ah well, she was going to die at some point'. Dr Johnson must be right in thinking he meant that she ought to have died at some later time, when a proper response to the news would be possible. It is this looking-forward to a time of peace in the future which makes him turn savagely against himself with 'To morrow, and to morrow, and to morrow'. He has ruined his own life by projecting himself into the imagination of future happiness, and this momentary glimpse of a quite impossible future—with his dead wife dying again at fitter time—shames him as an example of the unending dependence on a never-reached tomorrow. All progress towards those dreamy states are driftings without meaning. Shakespeare chooses other images for Macbeth's vision of life as utterly meaningless drifting, but all the same, what Macbeth is asserting is the impossibility of meaningful navigation, confounded and swallowed up by the storms which the weird sisters have engineered. The question that the tragedy leaves *us* with, is whether we, not having acted and suffered as Macbeth has done, allow ourselves to go on believing in navigation.

CHAPTER SIX—SHAKESPEARE (III): COMEDIES AND ROMANCES

'Not so much perdition as an hayre'

> *Gent.* 2. What, 'pray you, became of *Antigonus*, that carryed hence the Child?
>
> *Gent.* 3. Like an old Tale still, which will have matter to rehearse, though Credit be asleepe, and not an eare open; he was torne to pieces with a Beare: This avouches the Shepheards Sonne, who ha's not onely his Innocence (which seemes much) to justifie him, but a Hand-kerchief and Rings of his, that *Paulina* knowes.
>
> *Gent.* 1. What became of his Barke, and his Followers?
>
> *Gent.* 3. Wrackt the same instant of their Masters death, and in the view of the Shepheard; so that all the Instruments which ayded to expose the Child, were even then lost, when it was found.
>
> (*The Winter's Tale*, 5. 2. 59–72)

Shakespeare made extensive use of a shipwreck as a major structural device in his comedies and romances either to set the action of a play going or to create a redirection of the action. It is fundamental to a very early play, *The Comedy of Errors*, and to a very late play, *The Tempest*; it is important in *The Merchant of Venice, Twelfth Night, The Winter's Tale,* and *Pericles Prince of Tyre*. It is surprising how often these sea-disasters are insertions in or alterations of the source-material Shakespeare was using. It is surprising again how indifferent Shakespeare often seems to verisimilitude in introducing these shipwrecks. Obviously, shipwrecks in fiction have little to do with probability; they were standard examples of the unforeseen accident, of the unexpected intervention of fate or fortune or supernatural power in human designs, but even so Shakespeare seems sometimes almost to advertise his shipwrecks as authorial devices, as though he were courting the charge of unlikelihood. The shipwreck in *The Winter's Tale* is perhaps the boldest example of the author showing that he is at the helm.

There is no shipwreck in Greene's *Pandosto*, the source of *The Winter's Tale*, in which Leontes' disowned babe is set adrift in a boat. Shakespeare provided the ship, with Antigonus and the crew, in order to set the babe ashore in some desert place, and then had to destroy everyone in order to get rid of all witnesses to the whereabouts of Perdita. These are extraordinary lengths to go to, increasing the complications and improbabilities of the original story. *The Winter's Tale* as a whole is a series of scenes of great emotional power stitched together with ostentatiously crude narrative joins.[1] Shakespeare's purpose seems to have been to contrast the seeming-truth of stage-presentation with the fictionality of the narrative it depends on. Of the revival of the supposedly dead Hermione, Paulina says:

> That she is living,
> Were it but *told* you, should be hooted at
> Like a old Tale; but it *appeares* she lives . . .
> (5. 3. 115–17; my italics)

The ease with which a dramatist may send a ship and its crew to their doom in order to facilitate the progress of his story would seem to be at least a part of what Shakespeare is demonstrating when he gives the clown his extraordinary tragi-comic narrative, constantly sliding into farce, to relate the story of the devouring of Antigonus and the wreck of the ship that had brought him to the sea-coast of Bohemia.

1 See Philip Edwards, ' "Seeing is believing" ', in *Shakespeare and his Contemporaries*, ed. E. A. J. Honigmann, Manchester: Manchester University Press, 1986, pp. 79–93.

Clown. . . . But to make an end of the Ship, to see how the Sea flap-dragon'd it: but first, how the poore soules roared, and the sea mock'd them: and how the poore Gentleman roared, and the Beare mock'd him, both roaring lowder then the sea, or weather.

Shepherd. Name of mercy, when was this boy?

Clown. Now, now: I have not wink'd since I saw these sights: the men are not yet cold under water, nor the Beare halfe din'd on the Gentleman: he's at it now!

(3. 3. 97–106)

The disaster of the shipwreck in *The Winter's Tale* is a small but carefully inserted flagstone in the path towards the healing and restoration and rebirth with which the play ends. In the companion play, *The Tempest*, the shipwreck is also a device, but this time a device organized by the magus Prospero in order to bring about his own personal and political ends. It is not a 'real' shipwreck, but the illusion of one. 'We split! we split!', cry the sailors. Miranda saw the ship 'dash'd all to peeces' (1. 2. 8), and Prospero knows she saw it sink. But the ship is safely harboured, with the mariners in enchanted sleep beneath the hatches.

> There is no soule—
> No not so much perdition as an hayre
> Betid to any creature in the vessell
> Which thou heardst cry, which thou saw'st sinke.
>
> (1. 2. 29–32)

Prospero's magical device mirrors Shakespeare's artistic device; and the happy ending is what they jointly achieve, out of the initial violence of the shipwreck.

Shakespeare could hardly have foreseen the course of his writing career when in planning *The Comedy of Errors*, twenty years before composing *The Tempest*, he decided to nest the story which he took from Plautus' *Menaechmi* within

a romance frame of disaster at sea and restoration, but the
resemblances are prophetic.

In the *Menaechmi,* one of the twins was stolen from his
father in the market at Tarentum when he was seven years old,
and brought to Epidamnum, where the play is located.[2]
Neither of the parents of the twins appears in the play. *The
Comedy of Errors* is set in Ephesus, and the play opens with
the father, Egeon, who is searching for both his sons, relating
the story of a disaster in the past, when he and his wife, sailing
home from Epidamnum to Syracuse with their twin infant
sons, were shipwrecked and separated, each of them having
one of the twins in care. At the very end of the play, we learn
that the mother, Aemilia, became separated from *her* charge
and has spent the years in a priory at Ephesus, where she is
now the abbess. The entire family, father, mother, twin
brothers, are there reunited. This is the frame surrounding the
story of confusion which is the main substance of the play.

Shakespeare seems to have been determined to have Ephesus as the setting for his play, in spite of the difficulties it
created. The geography in the play is Adriatic, not Aegean.
The ports mentioned in Egeon's narrative are Syracuse,
Corinth, Epidamnum and Epidaurus. It will be seen from the
Ortelius map reproduced by R. A. Foakes in his Arden
edition that as well as the Epidaurus in the eastern Pelopon-
nese there was an Epidaurus on the Adriatic coast in 'Illyri-
cum' (modern Dubrovnik), north of Epidamnum, and this
must surely be the one Egeon mentions. The ship carrying him
and his family was wrecked in the Adriatic somewhere
between Epidamnum and the Gulf of Corinth. In Aemilia's
account of the rescue at the end of the play, she says that she
and the twin son in her care were taken out of the sea by sailors
from Epidamnum, but that fishermen from Corinth snatched
the infants (her son and one of the Dromios) and she had no
idea what became of them. She remained in the Epidamnum

2 See Bullough, I, pp. 13, 38.

ship. (See 5. 1. 350–55.) How then did the extraordinary coincidence come about that both she and those infants taken from her by the Corinthian fishermen ended up in Ephesus on the east coast of the Aegean? It would have been about 600 miles to Ephesus by sea; about 400 miles via Corinth.

> What then became of them, I cannot tell:
> I, to this fortune that you see mee in.

Nothing more is said about Aemilia's wanderings. Shakespeare wanted the mother to be abbess in a religious house in Ephesus, however she got there. Oddly enough, Shakespeare felt he should give some reason for the son getting to Ephesus. Antipholus of Ephesus tells the Duke that he was brought from Corinth 'by that most famous Warriour, / Duke *Menaphon*, your most renowned Unckle' (5. 1. 368–69). Renowned or not, this uncle makes no other appearance.

In adding to and altering the *Menaechmi*, Shakespeare drew on the story of Apollonius of Tyre, an ancient tale which had been re-told by John Gower in *Confessio Amantis* (1390). It is interesting that Gower referred to the mother as 'abbesse' in Diana's temple at Ephesus.[3] The Apollonius story contained a shipwreck (though it is quite distinct from the sea disaster in the play[4]), and it gave Shakespeare a missing mother, living as a priestess in a shrine, who is able in the end to bring together the sundered family. Ephesus was needed not only because it was there in the Apollonius story. Everyone knew of the worship of Diana at Ephesus, and of the work of Paul to establish the Christian community there, from the Acts of the Apostles, chapter XIX. Ephesus was strongly characterized not only as an important religious centre, both pagan and Christian, but (as described in the Acts) as a town of strange and dangerous enchantments, evil spirits, exorcists, men who used books to practise 'curious arts'.

3 *Ibid.*, VI, p. 418.
4 Muir (p. 18) is somewhat misleading in saying that the opening scene is derived from the Apollonius story.

The release of the twin brothers from the turmoil of confused identity, the freeing of Egeon from the threat of execution, the reunion of the long-divided family in the haven of the priory enable them as it were to continue the voyage interrupted by the shipwreck of long ago. However, the word used by the abbess-mother is not continuation but birth. 'After so long greefe such Nativitie' (5. 1. 407).

The Comedy of Errors has a kinship with *The Tempest* not only in depending on an initial shipwreck but in its uncharacteristic observance of the unities of time, place and action. It is also akin to another late romance, *Pericles Prince of Tyre*, which has no interest whatever in the unities, but which follows, much more closely, the Apollonius story.[5] A long time after the event, *Pericles* explains, as it were, why Shakespeare was so eager to have Ephesus as the reunion place for his sundered family in *The Comedy of Errors*, and it also explains, I think, why Shakespeare was so eager to provide shipwrecks as a prelude to salvation and restoration in so many plays.

* * * * *

The Merchant of Venice is the most important play between *The Comedy of Errors* and *Pericles* in featuring the interrupted voyage, but a significant and unnoticed prelude to that play is *A Midsummer Night's Dream*, the action of which also, in a sense, stems from a shipwreck. The love-potion which causes all the confusion in the forest comes into play because of the quarrel between Oberon and Titania over possession of the little Indian boy. Puck believed he was a changeling, stolen from an Indian king (2. 1. 22), but Titania gives a very different story. The boy's mother was her disciple; she died in giving birth to him, and Titania adopted him.

---

5 For Shakespeare's overall responsibility for *Pericles*, see my edition for the New Penguin Shakespeare (1976), p. 39. The play may well have been a collaboration, and the only text we have is much debased.

His mother was a Votresse of my Order,
And in the spiced *Indian* aire, by night
Full often hath she gossipt by my side,
And sat with me on *Neptunes* yellow sands,
Marking th'embarked traders on the flood,
When we have laught to see the sailes conceive,
And grow big bellied with the wanton winde:
Which she with pretty and with swimming gate
Following (her wombe then rich with my yong squire),
Would imitate, and saile upon the Land,
To fetch me trifles, and returne againe,
As from a voyage, rich with merchandize.
But she being mortall, of that boy did die,
And for her sake doe I reare up her boy,
And for her sake I will not part with him.

(2. 1. 123–37)[6]

Editors of the play deal woefully with 'th'embarked traders';
they agree that 'traders' means merchant-ships, and they leave
'embarked' unexplained. R. A. Foakes, in the New Cambridge edition, although noting that the *OED* has no use of
'traders' as trading ships before 1712, says that 'the sense is
unambiguous'. But, as always in Shakespeare, 'traders' means
people who trade, merchants, and 'embarked' has its usual
meaning. Of course, by metonymy, these merchants in their
ships become the ships themselves; and this metonymy came
into the language with 'merchantmen', first used for ships,
according to the *OED*, in 1627. Ironically, H. F. Brooks in
the Arden edition glosses 'traders' as 'merchantmen', thinking
apparently only of ships.

This humanization of the trading ships, so important in *The
Merchant of Venice*, is essential for the force of Titania's story,
bringing together ships and men and women: voyaging and
living. The Queen of the Fairies and her disciple must

6 Reading 'doe I' (Quarto) for the Folio's 'I doe' in line 136.

certainly have laughed at their conceit that these masculine ships with their swollen sails were like pregnant women. The ships are like the pregnant Indian woman, and she imitates the ships in going with her 'swimming gait' to fetch 'merchandise' for Titania. The analogies multiply. A ship returns from a voyage, 'rich with merchandise' secure in its hold; the Indian woman is rich with the baby in her womb. Her pregnancy is a voyage, and like so many ships, she is wrecked within sight of harbour: dies in giving birth. The Indian boy, so passionately desired by both Titania and Oberon, is the drowned treasure of the sea, rescued by and fought over by the gods.

The Merchant of Venice opens with a shipwreck, but it is a shipwreck of the imagination, a choric shipwreck, described by a minor character of indeterminate name, Salarino or Salerio. He supposes that Antonio's melancholy comes from his anxiety about his ships and all the wealth entrusted in them.

> Your minde is tossing on the Ocean,
> There where your Argosies with portly saile
> Like Signiors and rich Burgers on the flood,
> Or as it were the Pageants of the sea,
> Do over-peere the pettie Traffiquers
> That curtsie to them, do them reverence
> As they flye by them with their woven wings.
>
> (1. 1. 8–14)

As in *A Midsummer Night's Dream*, the ships are identified with the merchants—and these ships of Antonio's are singled out for the majesty of their wealth. It is of course the loss of this wealth to the sea that is the focal point of Salarino's fantasy.

> My winde cooling my broth
> Would blow me to an Ague, when I thought
> What harme a winde too great might doe at sea.
> I should not see the sandie houre-glasse runne,

But I should thinke of shallows, and of flats,
And see my wealthy *Andrew* docked in sand,
Vailing her high top lower then her ribs
To kisse her buriall; should I goe to Church
And see the holy edifice of stone,
And not bethinke me straight of dangerous rocks,
Which touching but my gentle Vessels side
Would scatter all her spices on the streame,
Enrobe the roring waters with my silkes,
And in a word, but even now worth this,
And now worth nothing?

(1. 1. 22–36)[7]

Salarino's words are the play's prologue, a poetic vision which embraces the play and works on a quite different level from Antonio's dry, rational contradiction of the peril—his ventures are distributed in several ships going to different places, and in any case, he adds, his 'whole estate' is not dependent 'upon the fortune of this present yeere'. This last remark is an interesting illustration of the different levels of realism in this play. Antonio flatly contradicts it when he says at the end of the scene, 'Thou knowst that all my fortunes are at sea'. Here he speaks on the same level as Salarino; all human fortune is at sea and in peril.

Antonio uses the riches for which he is venturing by means of his voyages to finance the venture of Bassanio, which is doubly described as a voyage. Bassanio actually goes by ship to Belmont (2. 6. 68 and 2. 8. 1), and his attempt to win Portia is compared to the voyage of the Argonauts to win the Golden Fleece (1. 1. 169–72; 3. 2. 241). The two men are united as high-risk adventurers: Antonio risking what Shylock calls 'the perrill of waters, windes, and rocks', and Bassanio the peril of the choice of caskets. In sealing to Shylock's bond, and offering his own flesh as security for the three thousand ducats

---

7 Reading 'docked' in line 27 for 'docks' (Q and F).

still at sea, Antonio further identifies himself with his ships
and his life with his merchandise. This identity, made plain in
Salarino's prologue and fundamental to Shakespeare's use of
voyage imagery, is reinforced by Gratiano's choric lines at 2.
6. 14.

> All things that are,
> Are with more spirit chased than enjoy'd.
> How like a younger or a prodigall
> The skarfed barke puts from her native bay,
> Hugg'd and embraced by the strumpet winde:
> How like the prodigall doth she returne,
> With over-wether'd ribs and ragged sailes,
> Lean, rent, and begger'd by the strumpet winde!
>   (2. 6. 12–19)[8]

The wind in Titania's speech was a wanton male, swelling up
the female sails; here it is a wanton female, debauching and
ruining a feckless young man. In both passages the voyage
ends badly. The Indian woman dies, the prodigal is ruined.

It was Shakespeare who made shipwreck the reason for the
forfeiture of the bond. There *is* a shipwreck in his source, *Il
Pecorone*, but it occurs in a different place in the narrative and
has nothing to do with the loan and the bond. There the bond
becomes forfeit because Gianetto, the Bassanio figure, revel-
ling in his new life with the lady, completely overlooks the day
for repayment.[9] But in *The Merchant of Venice* it is the
wrecking of all six of Antonio's ships, bringing home three
times the value of the bond, which makes repayment impossible. They are wrecked in all sorts of different places.

> But is it true *Salerio*?
> Hath all his ventures faild? what, not one hit?
> From Tripolis, from Mexico and England,

8 Quarto readings preferred in lines 14, 16, 17, 18.
9 Bullough, i, p. 471.

From Lisbon, Barbary, and India,
And not one vessell scape the dreadfull touch
Of Merchant-marring rocks?

                                        (3. 2. 266–71)

Shylock had wondered at the wide spread of Antonio's argosies, ventures 'squandred abroad' (1. 3. 18–21). Molly Mahood notes in her New Cambridge edition of the play (p. 13) that Antonio's trading enterprises go far beyond the actual range of Venetian activity at this time.[10] Shakespeare wanted world-wide voyaging by many ships and he wanted them all wrecked.

The central and the strongest stage-image of the play, which is properly named *The Merchant of Venice*, is of course that of Antonio with bared breast facing Shylock's knife. He has come to court from prison, stripped of the finery he wore as a rich burgher, emaciated, worn out—'lean, rent, and beg-ger'd'.

These greefes and losses have so bated mee,
That I shall hardly spare a pound of flesh . . .

                                        (3. 3. 32–33)

He spoke those words the day before. Now, 'I am a tainted Wether of the flocke, / Meetest for death' (4. 1. 114–15). For a fleeting moment, Shylock appears not as the demonized Jew out for revenge against the Gentiles, but as Atropos, ready to cut the thread of life of the wrecked world-wide voyager. *The Merchant of Venice* without Shylock is *Hamlet* without the Prince of Denmark, but the power of the Shylock story and the enigma of the Shylock figure must not blot out the strong element of fortune in the play. (The word occurs more frequently only in *Timon of Athens* and *Antony and Cleopatra*.) Antonio's endeavours are crowned with failure, Bas-sanio's with success, and both conclusions are as much a matter of luck as of judgement and desert.

10 The point is enlarged on by Gillies, pp. 55–56.

If Antonio's ruin is the result of a most astonishing run of
bad luck, his rescue and restoration are positively magical. At
one stroke he is free. Portia rules that under Venetian law,
flesh contains no blood, and Shylock's bond is therefore
meaningless. But Antonio regains not only his life and his
freedom, but his fortune, or the greater part of it. At the very
end of the play, at Belmont, Portia turns to him.

> *Anthonio* you are welcome,
> And I have better newes in store for you
> Then you expect: unseale this letter soone;
> There you shall finde three of your Argosies
> Are richly come to harbour sodainlie.
> You shall not know by what strange accident
> I chanced on this letter.
>
> (5. 1. 273–79)

The dramatist taketh away, and the dramatist giveth. It is the
profligacy which is so surprising. It took no fewer than six
shipwrecks to ruin Antonio. To have heard that *one* ship
managed to make harbour, or was falsely reported as lost,
would be reasonable, but this bland restoration of half the
sunken fleet seems a demonstration of unlikelihood. With so
much poetic investment within the play on the symbolism of
voyaging and the riches of merchandise and the pain of
shipwreck and loss, it is easy to feel cheated at the facile
outcome. Quiller-Couch was kinder than some in calling it
'this beautiful example of Shakespeare's dramatic impudence'.[11] It is curious, however, that this impudence should
relate to shipwrecks carefully inserted into the source-story,
and that the idea of 'the shipwreck that wasn't' should later be
elevated into the theme of an entire play. There is an analogue
to Portia's restoration of Antonio's fleet which does not seem
to have been noted. In Book I of the *Aeneid*, Aeneas bewails

11 Cambridge edition, p. 172.

the loss of the remainder of his fleet in the violent storm which has driven him on to the African shore. But his mother, the goddess Venus, announces to him the return of his comrades and the recovery of his fleet, borne into harbour by a change of wind. (*Namque tibi reduces socios classemque relatam / nuntio et in tutum versis Aquilonibus actam.*) Like Portia, she makes her source of information mysterious. *Ni frustra augurium vani docuere parentes.* The ships are safe—unless my parents were no good in teaching me the art of augury. (Neptune had organized the rescue of the ships.) As the one who can magically undo the past and restore what has been lost, Portia is helped by association with Venus to take her place alongside the magus Prospero, the abbess Aemilia, and the goddess Diana in *Pericles*. Portia's breathtaking restoration of Antonio's fleet is an indication of supernatural power at the same time that it is an indication of the dramatist's power. Shipwrecks, and their fortunate outcome, symbols of separation and of reunion, are also the displayed signs of the dramatist's life-and-death control of his characters.

In one of his most mature comedies, *Twelfth Night, or What You Will*, Shakespeare returned to the matter of *The Comedy of Errors*, confusions of identity between a pair of twins and the reunion of a divided family. And once again, to precipitate the action, he introduced a shipwreck. It is true that what is thought to be one of his main sources, Barnaby Riche's story of Silla and Apolonius,[12] contains a shipwreck, but it comes in a quite different part of the tale and does not involve the separation of brother and sister. Viola and Sebastian come from Messaline, an invented place, and Shakespeare does not think it worth mentioning where they were travelling to when their ship was wrecked. The play erupts into disruption: the past is effaced, the slate is cleansed. With a heavy sense of loss, Viola explores a new world: 'Conceale me

12 See Bullough, ii, pp. 344–63.

what I am'. The story of the play is a 'nativity', a chance-
medley in which brother and sister are reunited and enter into
new lives with new partners. The shipwreck is a kind of 'big
bang' to begin a process of recovery and renewal.

All the plays so far mentioned, early and late, are comedies.
It is not really helpful to separate the later ones as romances, as
we now tend to do; they are all romance-comedies. The ugly
duckling of the 'romances' is *Pericles Prince of Tyre*. I am
convinced that the play was designed and largely written by
Shakepeare, though the text we have is a debased, recon-
structed affair. More of its magic comes through in a good
performance in the theatre than in reading, but there are
passages which suggest the linguistic power of the lost
original. Even the original, however, must have been a very
unusual play for Shakespeare, with its episodic fortuitous
progress, and the deliberate air of medieval quaintness engineered by the figure of John Gower, the fourteenth-century
poet, who acts as presenter and explicator of the play. *Pericles*
is in fact one of two late plays in which Shakespeare hand-
somely acknowledged his debt to medieval story-tellers: here
to Gower, and in *The Two Noble Kinsmen* to Chaucer.

The Gower prologue and choruses are of great importance.
The prologue stresses the antiquity of the story—the better for
being antique—and its healing power over the centuries. It is
an appeal against the sophistication of 'these latter times' (1
Chorus, 11). The choruses not only recount those parts of a
long story which are not staged, but make the choice of what is
to be staged. Gower selects what he wants to *tell* and what he
wants to *show*.

> And what ensues in this fell storme
> Shall for it selfe, it selfe performe:
> I nill relate, action may
> Conveniently the rest convay,
> Which might not what by me is told.
> In your imagination hold

This Stage the Ship, upon whose Decke
The sea-tost *Pericles* appeares to speake.
(3 Chorus, 53–60)

This contrasting of telling and showing is a direct link with *The Winter's Tale*, with its insistence on the difference in credibility between the two genres. And by basing the scenes that are staged upon the creaking edifice of unlikely old tales, Shakespeare points to the gap between what is credible and what is true.

Shakespeare made many changes to the traditional names in the Apollonius story. For some of them it is hard to see the significance: but the change of the name of Pericles' daughter to Marina is clearly important. (In Gower she is Thaisa, and in Laurence Twine's *Patterne of Painefull Adventures*, a retelling of the Apollonius story which Shakespeare also used, she is Tharsia.) The play reiterates that she was born at sea, in a storm. 'My gentle babe *Marina*, / Whom, for she was borne at sea, I have named so' (3. 3. 12–13); 'Called *Marina* / For I was borne at sea' (5. 1. 155–56). 'Flesh of thy flesh, *Thaisa*, / Thy burden at the Sea, and call'd *Marina*, / For she was yeelded there' (5. 3. 46–48). When her father first sees her, he calls her 'this fresh new sea-farer'. As with Titania's Indian boy, when she was born her mother died (so it seemed). 'Aye me, poore maid, / Borne in a tempest, when my mother dide' (4. 1. 17–18).

In *Pericles* everything happens at sea, or by the sea. There are two main disasters. After the first, the shipwreck off Pentapolis, Pericles, the sole survivor, is thrown up naked and destitute, 'throng'd up with cold'. The fishermen give him a cloak. Then, in an incident which is not in the traditional story, a rusty armour is caught in the fishermen's nets; it is the armour which Pericles' father bequeathed to him, recovered from the wreck. 'The rough Seas . . . / Tooke it in rage', but, now calm, 'have given't againe'. Either this armour was jewelled, or jewels were washed up with it. For Pericles says:

By your furtherance I am cloth'd in Steele,
And spight of all the rapture of the Sea,
This Jewell holdes his buylding on my arme.
                    (2. 1. 154–56)[13]

Pericles wins the tournament and the hand of Thaisa. With the grant of treasure from the sea, 'part of my heritage' (2. 1. 123), he makes his new beginning, with marriage and the immediate conception of a child.

But a second time he is almost destroyed by the power of the sea, all this new fruitfulness taken away from him. He and Thaisa embark for Tyre, and they run into a violent storm. His wife goes into labour, gives birth to a daughter, but seems to die. She is placed in a satin-lined coffer, with jewels and rare spices about her, and cast into the sea, where

> . . . humming Water must orewelme thy corpes,
> Lying with simple shels.
>   (3. 1. 63–64)

When the chest is cast up on the coast of Ephesus, and Cerimon brings her back to life, those jewels placed with her are transmuted, and become her eyes.

>   Behold,
> Her ey-lids, cases to those heavenly jewels
> Which *Pericles* hath lost, begin to part
> Their fringes of bright gold. The Diamonds
> Of a most praysed water doth appeare,
> To make the world twise rich.
>   (3. 2. 97–102)

Pericles leaves the infant Marina to be brought up by Cleon and Dyoniza at Tarsus. Thaisa, believing that she will never see Pericles again, takes on a 'vestall liverie' and becomes a

---

13 The Quarto reads 'rupture of the Sea'. George Wilkins' prose version of the play, *The Painfull Adventures of Pericles Prince of Tyre*, gives us 'a Jewel, whom all the raptures of the sea could not bereave from his arme'.

'votaresse' in the temple of Diana at Ephesus, certain that she will 'never more have joy'. Pericles' deprivation is complete when he goes back to Tarsus to collect Marina and is told that she has died. Dionyza lies only about the circumstances of the death; she believes her murder-order has been carried out. 'Ile sweare shees dead,' the murderer had said to himself, 'and throwne into the Sea' (4. 1. 98–99).

It is to be revealed that two dead people, a wife and a daughter, are in fact still alive. It is obviously of the greatest importance that Pericles' discovery of Marina should take place aboard ship, and that in the harbour at Mytilene the citizens should be 'honoring of *Neptunes* triumphs' (5. 1. 17). This phrase occurs in a passage that is textually very insecure; the 'triumphs'—the common word for celebratory festivities or ceremonies—should be honouring Neptune. But the phrase as we have it, corrupt or not, emphasizes an essential point—that these triumphs are paying tribute to an all-conquering divinity.

Pericles' words to his daughter, if they are exactly his, are among the most mystical Shakespeare ever wrote.

> Oh come hither,
> Thou that begetst him that did thee beget;
> Thou that wast borne at sea, buried at *Tharsus*,
> And found at sea agen.
>
> (5. 1. 194–97)

Once again, as after the shipwreck, what was lost by 'the rapture of the sea' becomes a treasure restored. But the treasure that was lost was the wife. What is restored is the daughter. Before Pericles realizes who this strange young woman is, he has seen her as a kind of merged wife/daughter figure.

> My dearest wife was like this maid,
> And such a one my daughter might have beene.
> My Queenes square browes, her stature to an inch,

As wand-like straight, as silver voyst,
Her eyes as Jewell-like, and cased as richly . . .
                          (5. 1. 107–11)

Wife and daughter are taken from him by the sea (or by
Neptune); a wife-daughter figure, imaged as the lost treasure,
emerges from the sea, to revive and rejuvenate him from a state
of semi-existence—his hair and beard untrimmed for fourteen
years, and for three months unwashed, speaking to no one,
taking almost no sustenance. In all versions of the Apollonius
story, when Pericles has found his daughter, he is urged in a
vision to go to Ephesus. But only in Shakespeare is it the
goddess Diana who appears to Pericles (she makes altogether a
much stronger appearance in the play than in the sources).
Diana, the protectress of both wife and daughter, intervenes to
separate the composite wife-daughter figure into its two
persons. On making sacrifice at Diana's altar, Pericles and
Thaisa are reunited. Pericles blesses Diana for the vision, and
in the same speech tells Thaisa that Marina is to marry
Lysimachus in Pentapolis. The father is restored to his sexual
partner as the daughter finds hers. (This semi-miraculous
double-pairing is repeated in *The Winter's Tale*.)

Marina has more positive power, in relation to her father's
restoration, than either of her formidable rivals, Perdita and
Miranda. Years ago Wilson Knight pointed to the importance
of the references to art in connection with her.[14] Gower in his
chorus said that 'shee sings like one immortall', 'daunces as
Goddesse-like', and that in her needlework, 'her art sisters the
naturall Roses'. Pericles compared her with a palace 'for the
crownd truth to dwell in', and a statue of Patience, 'gazing on
Kings graves, and smiling / Extremitie out of act'. Marina, said
Knight, 'is, as it were, art incarnate'.

Knight believed that the last plays were intimations of
immortality and eternity. It seems to me that his identification
of Marina with the power of art leads in a very different

14 Knight (1947), pp. 62–65.

direction—towards dream rather than to a conception of ultimate reality. It is art which brings back the treasure which has been forfeited to the sea, art which pictures the gods as preservers as well as destroyers, art which straightens out the perversities of fortune. If Marina is indeed art incarnate, it is art that escapes from death, overcomes the enemies of chastity and restores the wounded prince.

Marina is one of several figures in the last plays who seem to shadow the work of the dramatist: both Time and Autolycus in *The Winter's Tale*, and of course Prospero in *The Tempest*. All these figures disrupt likelihood, change the course of things-as-they-are. Marina's dominance in the brothel is beyond belief.

> 1. But to have divinitie preach't there! Did you ever dreame of such a thing?
> 2. No, no. Come, I am for no more bawdie houses. Shall's goe heare the Vestalls sing?
> 1. Ile doe any thing now that is vertuous, but I am out of the road of rutting for ever.
>
> (4. 5. 4–9)

One might well say that one *could* only 'dream of such a thing'.

The Tempest is all dream—Prospero's dream, by which he creates a shipwreck to bring his enemies within his grasp and disable them, and then, undoing the shipwreck, provides for his return to Milan, with his issue to become kings of Naples. The shape of this dream was given to Shakespeare early on, in his reading of the Apollonius story in Gower's *Confessio Amantis*, and, from *The Comedy of Errors* onwards, ship-wreck and restoration became a main matrix for romance-comedies. Shipwreck symbolizes loss, deprivation, separ-ation—the condition towards which tragedies work, and from which comedies start.

Shipwreck is a powerful metaphor for defeat, suffering and loss. But even as the drowning seafarers cry out, Shakespeare indicates that it is his pen that has caused the wreck. There was no requirement for him to announce that shipwrecks were an author's device, but he does so, particularly in *The Winter's Tale*, and in *Pericles*, where shipwrecks are introduced as the stuff of old tales, such stuff as dreams are made on. By this insistence he provides a gateway for what is to come, signals that the work of restoration, undoing the past, reversing the irreversible, is a fantasy from the world of dreams. Puck's words conclude *A Midsummer Night's Dream*.

> If we shadowes have offended,
> Thinke but this (and all is mended)
> That you have but slumbred heere
> While these visions did appeare.
> And this weake and idle theame,
> No more yeelding but a dreame,
> Gentles, doe not reprehend.

The word 'shadow' is eloquent. It betokens actors, illusions, and *umbra*, the spectral forms of the dead. With the logic, not of the sea but of the writing desk, that if you can wreck a ship at any time, you can at any time undo the damage, the dead are brought back to life, and act out what might have been. What is then important is to build on these sands of make-believe edifices of power, palaces for the crowned truth to dwell in. The image of restoration is the recovery of lost treasure, the jewel cast up by the sea. The air is holy, the place sacred— Ephesus indeed. Presiding over the restoration is a woman. Portia and Paulina are temporarily invested with more than natural powers; Aemilia is the abbess in a religious house, Diana a goddess. Only in *The Tempest* is the thaumaturge a male.

Demonstrating to the full the theatre's power to create reality, the romance-comedies declare it to be illusion. They display the strength of our longing, the beauty of what we long for, the holy joy of recovering what we have lost, and the impossibility of it all.

PART THREE

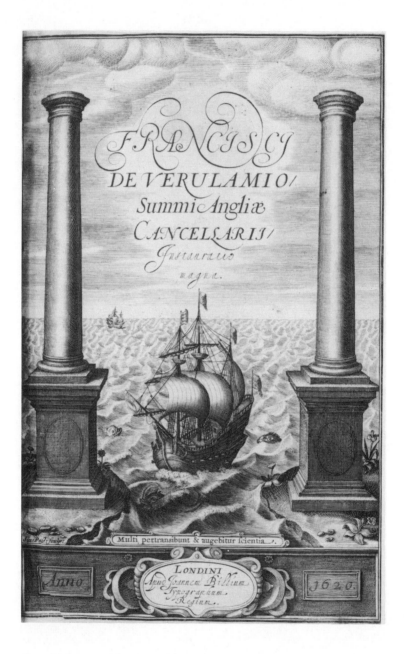

Francis Bacon, title-page of *Instauratio Magna*, 1620, engraved by Simon Passe

CHAPTER SEVEN—BACON
'The Art it Selfe of
Invention and Discoverie'

And like as the *West Indies* had never been discovered, if the use of the Mariners Needle had not been first discovered, though the one be vast Regions, and the other a small Motion; So it cannot be found strange, if Sciences bee no further discovered, if the Art it selfe of *Invention* and *Discoverie*, hath been passed over.

> *The Advancement of Learning*, 1605,
> Bk. II [iii, p. 384].[1]

In his writings Francis Bacon was constantly associating the progress of knowledge with voyaging.[2] The association was most strongly affirmed in the title-page of the *Instauratio Magna* of 1620, which shows two ships sailing through the Pillars of Hercules (the Straits of Gibraltar) with the motto from the Book of Daniel (12:4), 'Multi pertransibunt et augebitur scientia', which Bacon was always quoting (in different renderings). 'Manie shall passe too and fro, and science shalbe increased' is the version given in *Valerius Terminus: Of the Interpretation of Nature* (1603). Interestingly, Simon Passe's engraving (see opposite) shows two ships which seem to be returning from the open sea towards the reader. Either they are meant to be bringing back their cargo of knowledge from afar, or else Passe, with or without Bacon's approval, has given the reader a god's eye view of

1 Quotations from Bacon's English writings are normally from the first editions; for consistency, however, all references are to the standard edition of the Works by Spedding, Ellis, and Heath, 14 vols, 1857–74 (reprinted 1962–63). These references are placed within square brackets.

2 See Vickers, pp. 183–86, Cawley, pp. 131–32, pp. 242–49, Rennie, pp. 43–49.

ships about to emerge from the Mediterranean sea of medieval
timidity into the unknown. Whichever way they are going,
they have broken through, or they are about to break through
the pillars of Hercules, which antiquity regarded as the proper
boundary of human searching. Adopting the motto of the
emperor Charles V (1500–58), Bacon wrote, 'these times may
justly beare in their word . . . *Plus ultrà* in precedence of the
ancient *Non ultrà*'.[3] The pillars of Hercules were the 'columns
of no further proceeding', *columnae tanquam fatales*, which
men must learn were not the true boundaries of mental effort.
'Why should a fewe received Authors stand up like *Hercules
Columnes*, beyond which, there should be no sayling, or
discovering?'[4]

Sailing through the Pillars of Hercules into the open sea was
Bacon's symbol for the redirection of the intellectual energy of
mankind which he spent his life advocating: the 'great instauration' which would give to the human race understanding of
and power over nature, and immeasurably improve the
conditions of life on earth. The great instauration was at the
same time restoration, fulfilment, and revolution; returning
mankind to the knowledge and power possessed by Adam
before the Fall, realizing both biblical prophecy and the
intimations of the ancients, but above all making a new
beginning in defiance of current intellectual endeavour.[5]

The effort to liberate mankind, through the medium of his
writings, was itself seen as a voyage. First, a coasting voyage
investigating what was so far known: *Itaque scientiarum atque
artium receptarum oras legere* ['We will therefore make a
coasting voyage along the shores of received arts and

3 *Advancement of Learning*, Bk. II [iii, p. 340]. See further in Earl
Rosenthal's article in *Journal of the Warburg and Courtauld Institute*, 34
(1973), 198–230.

4 *Filum Labyrinthi* [iii, p. 498]; *Instauratio Magna* [1,125]; *Advancement of Learning*, Bk II [iii, 321].

5 Charles Whitney gives an excellent analysis of the implications of
'instauration' in *Francis Bacon and Modernity*, 1986.

sciences']. And then, into the open sea: *Porro praetervecti artes veteres, intellectum humanum ad trajiciendum instruemus* ['Then, having sailed past the ancient arts, we shall equip the human intellect for passing beyond'].[6] This is from the *Instauratio Magna* of 1620. In the 1605 *Advancement of Learning*, the initial coasting voyage had been described as in itself a round-the-world voyage.

> Thus have I made as it were a small Globe of the Intellectual world, as truly and faithfully as I coulde discover, with a note and description of those parts which seeme to mee, not constantly occupate, or not well converted by the labour of Man.[7]

This is indeed the language of the returning navigator. 'Discover' is used here in its very common sense of 'explore'. Here is a map, he writes, as accurate as my exploration is able to make it, noting all the places hitherto unknown or undeveloped.

The most forceful of all the structural voyage-images in Bacon's writings is of course in the late 'science fiction', *New Atlantis*. In a very positive and tangible way, voyages of discovery provided wholly new knowledge about our world. In *New Atlantis* a voyage of discovery lights upon an unknown island in the South Sea where all new areas of research and technology have been investigated and exploited just as Bacon desired. Bacon has set up his programme of revolutionary intellectual redirection within a discovery metaphor. *New Atlantis* is a fable of the discovery of discovery: the geographical discovery of intellectual discovery. Perceiving the metaphor enhances the power of the opening.

> So that finding our selves in the Midst of the greatest Wildernesse of Waters in the World, without Victual, we gave our Selves for lost Men, and prepared for Death.

6 'The Plan of the Work', preceding *Instauratio Magna* [i, pp. 134–35].
7 *Advancement of Learning*, Bk II [iii, p. 490].

But God came to their aid and they reached the mysterious island of Bensalem, whereon they found Salomon's House, 'the noblest foundation . . . that ever was upon the earth', whose end was 'the Knowledge of *Causes*, and Secrett Motions of Things; And the Enlarging of the bonds of *Humane Empire*, to the Effecting of all Things possible'.[8]

Historically speaking, the 'plus ultra' of Bacon's figure of speech had already happened. For over a hundred years the unknown seas had been traversed, and immense areas of the world's surface, unknown to Europeans, had been revealed. Bacon's writings constantly allude to these discoveries: to Columbus, to Ortelius' maps, to the possibility of a Southern Continent.[9] He gloried in these achievements of his age. Antiquity knew little about the earth, whereas 'in our time . . . both many parts of the New World and the limits on every side of the Old World are known, and our stock of experience has increased to an infinite amount'.[10]

Time and again, Bacon referred to the successes of voyages of discovery as major achievements in themselves in the struggle to advance human knowledge, and, just as important, as a sign that this was the age appointed for the opening up of the frontiers of knowledge in every sphere. We find the thought several times in *Valerius Terminus* and several times in the *Advancement of Learning*, and also in *Novum Organum*. Most eloquently in the passage on the History of Cosmography in the *Advancement*.

> And this Proficience in Navigation, and discoveries, may plant also an expectation of the furder proficience, and augmentation of all Scyences, because it may seeme they

8 *New Atlantis* [iii, pp. 129, 145, 156]. There is a good account of the book in Rennie, 43–49.

9 *Advancement of Learning* [iii, pp. 291, 408]; *Parasceve* [i, p. 402]. See Cawley, 242–49, for a full account of Bacon's use of voyage literature, especially in *Sylva Sylvarum*.

10 *Novum Organum*, Bk I, lxxii [i, p. 182).

are ordained by God to be *Coevalls*, that is, to meete in one Age. For so the Prophet *Daniel* speaking of the latter times foretelleth: *Plurimi pertransibunt, et Multiplex erit Scientia:* as if the opennesse and through passage of the world, and the encrease of knowledge were appointed to be in the same ages.[11]

It would be a disgrace if the sign were to be ignored, if 'while the regions of the material world—that is, of the earth, and of the sea, and of the stars,—have been in our times laid widely open and revealed, the intellectual globe should remain shut up within the narrow limits of old discoveries (*globi autem intellectualis fines inter veterum inventa et angustias cohibeantur*).[12]

The recent geographical discoveries are seen as part of a vastly greater expansion of universal knowledge which they herald. It is but a small step to see them as a symbol of that expansion of which they are a contributing part and the vanguard. The progress towards metaphor can be seen in *Valerius Terminus*.

The new found world of land was not great*er* addition to the ancient Continent then there remayneth at this daie a worlde of inventions and sciences unknowne, havinge respecte to those that are knowne, with this difference, that the ancient Regions of knowledge will seeme as barbarous compared with the new, as ye new regions of people seeme barbarous compared to manie of the old.[13]

So the voyage-metaphor in Bacon, used as it almost solely is in the context of the advancement of knowledge, has this special force, which Coleridge thought to be an essential quality of a symbol, that it partakes of the reality to which it refers. In

11 *Advancement of Learning*, Bk II [iii, p. 340].
12 *Novum Organum*, Bk I, lxxxiv [i, p. 191].
13 *Valerius Terminus*, British Library MS Harl. 6463, pp. 14–15 [iii, p. 323]. On Bacon's use of the early voyages, see Franklin, 7–9.

criticizing the philosophy of the past for concentrating too much on final causes to the exclusion of secondary or physical causes, Bacon writes that Plato 'ever ancreth uppon that shoare'. Teleological theories are '*Remoraes* and hinderances to stay and slugge the Shippe from furder sayling'. Final causes should be 'kept within their owne province'; as it is, 'their excursions into the limits of *Phisicall causes,* hath bred a vastnesse and solitude in that tract'. (That is to say, like a foreign competing fleet, they have occupied a part of the ocean which they do nothing with, and keep out the ships of other nations which could use it for trade and empire.)[14]   This 'final causes' passage shows an unusually extended series of voyage-images. An interesting example of the use of sea-imagery to illustrate method in scientific advancement occurs in *Valerius Terminus*. It has to do with the 'kenning'—the stretch of water you can see from a ship at any one time. *Valerius Terminus: Of the Interpretation of Nature* was never completed and never published. The passage in question was meant to follow an ambitious 'Inventorie or an enumeration and view of inventions already discovered and in use'—of which only a tiny fragment exists. The nature and kinds of these inventions, he writes, 'have bene described as they could be discovered; for your eye cannot passe one kenning without further saylinge'.[15] It is the consecutiveness of scientific discovery which Bacon is here talking about (as so often). One discovery leads to another. You cannot describe discoveries all together; you have to proceed from one to the next to understand how it works. Surveying the sea of knowledge, Bacon now moves from ship to shore. 'Only we have stood upon the best advantages of the notions received, as upon a mounte, to shewe the knowledges adjacent and confyninge.'

Insistence upon the consecutiveness of scientific discovery is one of the reasons why Bacon was constantly referring to the

14 *Advancement of Learning*, Bk II [iii, p. 358].
15 *Valerius Terminus*, p. 18 [iii, p. 325].

discovery of the mariner's compass. Famously, he said that if it was glory for a man to invent something which benefited the whole human race, how much greater was the glory of inventing that by means of which all else could be invented.[16] The ship's compass he thought an ideal example of an invention which could generate further and further discoveries.

> But as in former ages when men sailed only by obser-
> vation of the stars, they could indeed coast along the
> shores of the old continent or cross a few small and
> mediterranean seas; but before the ocean could be
> traversed and the new world discovered [*novi orbis
> regiones detegerentur*] , the use of the mariner's needle
> [*acus nauticae*], as a more faithful and certain guide, had
> to be found out; in like manner the discoveries which
> have been hitherto made in the arts and sciences are such
> as might be made by practice, meditation, observation,
> argumentation,—for they lay near to the senses, and
> immediately beneath common notions; but before we can
> reach the remoter and more hidden parts of nature, it is
> necessary that a more perfect use and application of the
> human mind and intellect be introduced.[17]

In praising the mariner's needle for the same reasons in the *Advancement of Learning*, written some years before the above passage, Bacon defined the generative power of the compass as conferring *direction*.

> And secondly, that those *experiments* be not onely
> esteemed which have an immediate and present use, but
> those principally which are of most universall conse-
> quence for invention of other experiments, and those
> which give most light to the Invention of causes; for the
> Invention of the Mariners Needle, which giveth the

16 *Novum Organum*, Bk I, cxxix [i, p. 222].
17 Preface to *Instauratio Magna* (Spedding's translation) [i, pp. 129–30].

direction, is of noe lesse benefit for Navigation, then the
invention of the sailes which give the Motion.[18]

The physical direction of the ship by the compass to send it out
to discover unknown lands is a perfect image for the enabling
methods of the new inductive science laid out in *Novum
Organum*. To head in the right direction seemed to Bacon
more important than obtaining results. 'The Master in the
Shippe, is judged by the directing his course aright, and not by
the fortune of the Voyage.'[19]

       *   *   *   *   *

The importance to Bacon of the voyage as an image of the
quest for new knowledge is shown admirably in his use of the
word 'discovery'. We should begin with the opening of *New
Atlantis*. Lost in the South Sea, the mariners prepared for
death (see above, p.153).

> Yet we did lift up our Harts and Voices to GOD
> above, who *sheweth his Wonders in the Deepe*; Beseech-
> ing him of his Mercy, that as in the *Beginning* He
> discovered the *Face* of the *Deepe*, and brought forth *Dry-
> Land*, So he would now discover Land to us, that we
> moght not perish. And it came to passe, that the next Day
> about Evening, we saw within a Kenning before us,
> towards the North, as it were thick Cloudes, which did
> put us in some hope of Land . . .[20]

The first use of 'discover' in this passage looks strange: God
'discovered the face of the deep, and brought forth dry land'.
Bacon's editors, Ellis and Spedding, found the word a
problem: 'If *discover* be the right word, it must mean *removed
the covering of* the face of the deep'. At this point in Genesis,
the King James Bible reads: 'And God said, Let the waters

18 *Advancement of Learning*, Bk II [iii, p. 363].
19 *Ibid*., Bk II [iii, p. 371].
20 *New Atlantis* [iii, p. 129].

under the heaven be gathered together unto one place, and let the dry land appear'. So Ellis and Spedding were right; God removed a covering and revealed what he had placed there. It is as though Bacon is putting the word through strange grammatical paces in order to demonstrate its full implications. For him, the basic meaning of the word 'discover' was to remove the covering of ignorance, and reveal the secrets of God. He quoted Democritus in the *Advancement*: 'The truthe of Nature lyeth hidde in certaine deepe Mynes and Caves'.[21] In the *Novum Organum* he quoted Solomon: 'It is the glory of God to conceal a thing; the glory of a king to find it out.'[22] The first book of the *Advancement* is devoted to justifying the searching out of the secrets of God. Discovery is the removal of ignorance, and the revealing of what has been there all the time.

In the first sentence of this *New Atlantis* passage, God is twice the subject of the verb 'discover'. The object of the verb on the first occasion is the lid; on the second occasion the object is what lies inside: 'So he would now discover Land to us'. Discovery by human beings is directed by God; it is the uncovering of his own secrets.

The word 'discover' was quite often used by Bacon in the neutral sense of 'expose' or 'disclose'—as at the close of the essay 'Of Adversitie', which I shall shortly be discussing: '*Prosperity* doth best discover Vice; But *Adversity* doth best discover Vertue'. But, as we have seen, he also frequently uses the word in the sense that had become firmly established in English in the latter half of the sixteenth century, meaning exploring for and finding new lands and seas—as for example in Sir Humphrey Gilbert's *Discourse* on the North-West Passage, written in 1566 and published in 1576.[23] 'All these commodities would grow by following this our dis-

21 *Advancement of Learning*, Bk II [iii, p. 351].
22 *Novum Organum*, Bk I,cxxix [i, p. 221].
23 Hakluyt, vii, pp. 158–90.

covery . . .' So Bacon speaks of 'this Proficience in Navigation, and discoveries' (see above, p. 154), and 'no sayling, or discovering' (p. 152). It does not seem, however, that the word was in use in his time as regards new findings in the intellectual or scientific sphere. The *Oxford English Dictionary* has no examples before 1670. If one looks at Bacon's use of the word 'discovery', one can see him reaching out from its geographical sense to a scientific context. 'Discovery' in respect of the workings of nature is a metaphor imported from voyages of discovery.

Bacon's actual vocabulary is made rather hazy for us in this context because we normally read his Latin works in the standard English translation of Ellis and Spedding. And this is peppered with the word 'discovery'. In the passage which heads this chapter, Bacon (writing in English) uses 'discovered' and 'discovery' four times, once in a territorial context and three times in a scientific context. The translation from Bacon's later Latin version of this, in *De Augmentis Scientiarum* (Book V, chapter 2), understandably uses 'discovered' and 'discovery' as they are found in the English version. But the Latin runs as follows:

> Atque sicut India Occidentalis nunquam nobis inventa fuisset nisi praecessissit acus nauticae inventio, licet regiones illae immensae, versoriae motus pusillus sit; ita non est cur miretur quispiam in Artibus perlustrandis et promovendis ampliores progressus factos non esse, quandoquidem Ars ipsa Inveniendi et Perlustrandi Scientias hactenus ignoretur.[24]

The words used for 'discover/y' are 'invenire', 'inventio' (finding out) and 'perlustrandus' (surveying thoroughly). We find elsewhere such phrases as 'Novus Orbis . . . nunc primum reperta'[25] (the New World now for the first time

24 Works, i, p. 617.
25 *Ibid.*, i, p. 216.

discovered), where 'reperire' (to find out) is used; 'novi orbis regiones detegeruntur'[26] (regions of the new world were discovered), where 'detegere' (to expose, lay bare) is used. As regards scientific discoveries, the normal word is 'invenire' or its derivatives: 'inventor' (one who finds out), 'inventio' (a discovery), 'inventum' (a new procedure of device).

So we exclude Bacon's Latin, or rather translations from it, in a consideration of his use of the word 'discovery'. We need to turn to the earliest work in English in which he outlined his programme for human learning: *Valerius Terminus: Of the Interpretation of Nature*, which probably dates from 1603. Here we find Daniel's prophecy quoted: 'Manie shall passe too and fro, and science shalbe increased; as if the opening of the world by navigation and comerce and the further discovery of knowledg should meete in one time or age'.[27] This is the first use of 'discovery' in the intellectual or scientific sense that I can find in Bacon, and it occurs in the context of voyaging and exploration. A few paragraphs later, in an important passage speaking of the true end of knowledge, he writes: 'to speake plainly and clearely it is a discovery of all operations and possibilities of operations from immortalitie (if it were possible) to the meanest mechanicall practize'.[28] This, which is a definition of the true end of knowledge, is also a definition of 'discovery' in its transferred sense: the finding out of what is unknown, for the benefit of mankind. As he puts it a little later, again with this air of definition: 'the true end, scope, or office of knowledge . . . I have set downe to consist not in anie plausible, delectable, reverend, or admired discourse, . . . but in effecting and workinge, and in discovery of particulers not revealed before for the better indowment and helpe of mans life'.[29] *Valerius Terminus* was not published. It was superseded by *The Two Books of the Proficience*

26 *Ibid.*, i, p. 129.
27 *Valerius Terminus*, p. 10 [iii, p. 221].
28 *Ibid.*, pp. 12–13 [iii, p. 222]. (Spedding reads 'process' for 'practize'.)
29 *Ibid.*, p. 30 [iii, p. 233].

and Advancement of Learning of 1605. In the *Advancement* we find two notable passages in which the word 'discovery' is used in a scientific sense in a context of voyaging which seems to be there to provide the word with emotional force. One is the passage quoted at the head of this chapter. The other comes earlier in Book II. Writing of unorganized and opportunistic experiments, he agrees that there have been many inventions—

> But these are but Coastings along the shoare, *Premendo littus iniquum.* For it seemeth to me, there can hardly bee discovered any radicall or fundamentall alterations, and innovations in Nature, either by the fortune and essayes of experiments, or by the light and direction of Phisical causes.[30]

The word most often used in the *Advancement* for new scientific ideas and theories is not 'discovery' but 'invention'. In the all-important 'West Indies' passage at the head of this chapter, 'invention' and 'discovery' are synonymous: 'the Art it selfe of *Invention* and *Discoverie* hath been passed over'. In his section on the Arts Intellectual in Book II of the *Advancement*, Bacon does his best to wrest the word 'invention' from its dominant current usage, in connection with the selection of arguments for asserting and maintaining known positions, and assign it instead to break-throughs in knowledge.

> INVENTION is of two kindes much differing; The one, of ARTS and SCIENCES, and the other of SPEECH and ARGUMENTS. The former of these, I doe report deficient; which seemeth to me to be such a deficience, as if in the making of an Inventorie, touching the State of a defunct, it should be set downe, *That there is no readie money.* For as money will fetch all other commodities; so this knowledge is that which should purchase all the rest. And

30 *Advancement of Learning*, Bk II [iii, p. 361].

like as the *West Indies* had never been discovered, if the
use of the Mariners Needle had not been first discovered;
though the one be vast Regions, and the other a small
Motion; So it cannot be found strange, if Sciences bee no
further discovered, if the Art it selfe of *Invention* and
Discoverie, hath been passed over.[31]

Invention in its second (and normal) acceptation—finding out
the best terms in which to argue a case—is ruled out as
improper.

The *Invention* of speech or argument, is not properly an
Invention: for to *Invent* is to discover that we know not,
and not to recover or resummon that which wee alreadie
knowe.[32]

'To *Invent* is to discover that we know not'; the words are to
be synonymous.[33] We have to forget (for this period) the
distinction made by Blair in 1783 and cited in the *OED*. 'We
invent things that are new; we discover what was before
hidden. Galileo invented the telescope; Harvey discovered the
circulation of the blood.' When we read sixteenth-century
writers on new findings about the processes of nature, where
we would expect 'discover' or 'discovery' we usually find
'invent' or 'invention'. A manuscript note made by Nicholas
Hill in the early seventeenth century concerning William
Warner speaks of 'Mr Warrener the inventor probably of the
circulation of the blood, of which subject he made a treatise
consisting of two books which he sent to Dr Harvey . . .'.[34]

31 *Ibid.* [iii, p. 384].
32 *Ibid.* [iii, p. 389].
33 It seems to me unfortunate that at the beginning of her book on
Bacon's relationship with contemporary logic and rhetoric, Lisa Jardine
should say that throughout his work Bacon stresses the distinction between
'discovery' and 'invention'. On the contrary, he insisted on the identity of
the two words. See Jardine, 6.
34 See Jean Jacquot, in Shirley, 120.

When in 1610 Sir William Lower wrote to Thomas Harriot about his 'discoverie' of certain stars with his 'Cylinder', he was using the word in its geographical sense.[35] But when the motion of the stars was the issue, the word is 'invent' where we would expect 'discover', as in Richard Bostocke in 1585, praising Copernicus, but saying that he is not to be called 'the author and inventor of the motions of the starres, which long before were taught by *Ptolomeus* . . .'.[36] So Bacon had a perfectly good word for an innovatory insight or theory concerning the working of the natural world, and that word was 'invention' (which did not then mean the creation of a new technical tool or process). But, in addition to that, he liked to use a voyage metaphor, a figure of speech deriving from voyages of exploration: the word 'discovery'. Thereby the work of the scientist in finding out the workings of nature is actually dignified by being made parallel to the work of intrepid seamen finding out new oceans and new lands. Because the finding out of new oceans and new lands was itself a contribution to the increased understanding of the natural world, 'discovery' in the scientific context is not so much metaphor as synecdoche—using a part for the whole. The great value of transferring the word from a particular geographical use to a general scientific use is that it establishes what was for Bacon its primary meaning, which he pedantically insisted on in that strange passage at the beginning of *New Atlantis*: uncovering, with God's aid, that which God for his own good reasons has kept concealed.

It may not be immediately obvious how daring Bacon was at this dawning stage of empirical science to label any new theory about the working of nature a 'discovery'. 'Discovery' is a retrospective term: it means finding out that which we have confirmed by later verification. It was all right for land, because that was palpably *there*. But to call a theory, whether

35 See Edward Rosen, in Shirley, 11.
36 Quoted in Johnson, 183.

of the circulation of the blood or the circulation of the planets, a *discovery*, with the status of a revelation of God's mysteries, when there were such slender means of independent verification, was optimism indeed. Bacon's own notorious uncertainty about the positive scientific advances of his own day is ironic testimony to the daring of his own nomenclature—his invention of discovery.

*   *   *   *   *

Although in a notable study of Bacon's Essays[37] Stanley Fish argued that 'there has been a general recognition in the twentieth century of the close relationship between Bacon's *Essays* and his scientific program', it is a sign of their different concerns that, though written over such a long period of Bacon's life, the Essays contain no significant voyage-imagery at all. They have no need for it. There is, however, one major exception—the late essay, 'Of Adversitie', first published in 1625. This short, complex, difficult work throws a strange light backwards on the voyage imagery which has dominated the scientific writing, and places it in a moving context of Bacon's moral and religious beliefs. Fish's study, brilliant in so many ways, does not serve this profound essay well in the six or seven pages devoted to analysing it. The great merit of Fish's approach to the Essays was his demonstration of their obliquity and cunning, their constant trapping of the reader into assenting to propositions which are then undermined. Fish rightly insisted on Bacon's contempt for the bland formulations of customary rhetorical exposition, and the remarkable way in which his own strategy constantly misleads, confuses and unsettles the reader. But to what end is all this? Fish would have us believe that disturbing the reader was all that Bacon was after. 'The question of what "adversity" is has no more been settled here than the question of what "love" is was settled in that essay' (p. 101). It seems to me that

37 Fish, p. 78–155 ('The Experience of Bacon's *Essays*').

Bacon's great cunning in this essay is directed to a much more purposeful and important end than simply bewildering his readers—though it does that too.

It was an high speech of *Seneca*, (after the manner of the Stoickes) *That the good things, which belong to Prosperity, are to be wished; but the good things, that belong to Adversity, are to be admired. Bona Rerum Secundarum, Optabilia; Adversarum, Mirabilia.* Certainly if Miracles, be the Commaund over Nature, they appeare most in Adversity. It is yet a higher speech of his, then the other, (much too high for a Heathen) *It is true greatnesse, to have in one, the Frailty of a Man, and the Security of a God. Verè magnum, habere Fragilitatem Hominis, Securitatem Dei.* This would have done better in Poesy; where Transcendences are more allowed. And the Poets indeed, have beene busy with it; For it is, in effect, the thing, which is figured in that Strange Fiction, of the Ancient Poets, which seemeth not to be without mystery; Nay, and to have some approach, to the State of a Christian: that *Hercules, when he went to unbinde Prometheus,* (by whom Human Nature is represented) *sailed the length of the great Ocean, in an Earthen Pot, or Pitcher:* Lively describing Christian Resolution; that saileth, in the fraile Barke of the Flesh, thorow the Waves of the World. But to speake in a Meane. The Vertue of *Prosperitie,* is Temperance; The Vertue of *Adversity* is Fortitude: which in Morals is the more Heroicall Vertue. *Prosperity* is the Blessing of the Old Testament; *Adversity* is the Blessing of the New; which carrieth the greater Benediction, and the Clearer Revelation of Gods Favour. Yet, even in the old Testament, if you Listen to *Davids* Harpe, you shall heare as many Herselike Ayres, as Carols: And the Pencill of the holy Ghost, hath laboured more, in describing, the Afflictions of *Job,* then the Felicities of *Salomon. Prosperity* is not without many Feares and

Distastes; and *Adversity* is not without Comforts and Hopes. Wee see in Needle-workes, and Imbroideries, It is more pleasing, to have a Lively Worke, upon a Sad and Solemne Ground; then to have a Darke and Melancholy Worke, upon a Lightsome Ground: Judge therefore, of the Pleasure of the Heart, by the Pleasure of the Eye. Certainly, Vertue is like pretious Odours, most fragrant, when they are incensed, or crushed: For *Prosperity* doth best discover Vice; But *Adversity* doth best discover Vertue.[38]

The centre of the essay is the strange legend that the sufferings of Prometheus were relieved by Hercules, who came to his rescue by sailing across the ocean in a pitcher, and the association of this legend with the dictum of Seneca that it is true greatness to have at the same time the frailty of man and the security (or freedom from anxiety) of a god.[39] Both the legend and the dictum had been in Bacon's mind for many years. Seneca's saying appeared in *The Advancement of Learning* in 1605, in a discussion on the state of moral philosophy, 'that knowledge which considereth of the APPETITE and WILL of Man' [iii. 417–18]. On the question of 'the EXEMPLAR Or PLATFORME of GOOD', Bacon argues that the 'infinite disputations' of the ancients regarding the supreme good or felicity or beatitude were concerned with what was essentially 'the heathen Divinity', and in these times 'are by the christian faith discharged': that is to say, are rendered null and void by the truths of Christianity, which

38 *Essayes*, 1625, pp. 22–24.
39 There is a learned disquisition on the sources and analogues of the Hercules legend in R. S. Peterson's *Imitation and Praise in the Poems of Ben Jonson*, 1981, chapter 3. (John Pitcher calls attention to this in the Penguin edition of the Essays.) Peterson reproduces a picture of a Greek vessel of the fifth century BC, showing Hercules with his lion skin and knobbly club sailing in a bowl, for all the world like one of the three wise men of Gotham.

place our felicity in the hope of a future world after death. This 'doctrine of the Philosophers heaven', from which we as Christians have been freed, 'fayned an higher elevation of mans Nature then was; (For we see in what an height of stile *Seneca* writeth, *Vere Magnum, habere fragilitatem hominis, securitatem Dei)'.*[40]

The 'height of style' refers to the character of what Seneca is saying rather than to his phraseology. Seneca is accused of presumption, or at least audacity, in so over-valuing human nature that he claims the 'security' of a god can coexist with the frailty of the flesh. ('Security' in English at this time had the same primary meaning as the Latin *securitas*: viz, freedom from care, composure, unconcern.) This is heathen hubris, now chastened by Christian knowledge. But to know why Bacon thought this saying of Seneca, which (in his usual fashion) he misquotes, is so 'high' or arrogant, we have to take in its context—which is that of a voyage. In his *Epistolae*, number 53, Seneca wrote to Lucilius about a short sea-journey he had made. The weather turned bad and he felt very sea-sick, so he persuaded the helmsman to put him ashore. He goes on to reflect how little we are conscious of our weakness until we are hit by some unmistakable disorder. With physical complaints, awareness comes quickly enough, as with sea-sickness. But with afflictions of the spirit, we may continue to remain in obtuse unawareness of our condition. The value of the study of philosophy is that it makes you fully conscious of your weakness— and teaches you the way to cure yourself. If you devote yourself entirely to philosophy, Seneca continues, you will move ahead of the rest of mankind. In fact, you won't be far behind the gods. They of course have the advantage that they live longer (*diutius erunt*). But in one respect doesn't a wise man surpass the gods? The god has his wisdom from nature, the wise man from his own efforts. *Ecce res magna, habere imbecillitatem hominis, securitatem dei.* Look at that

40 *Advancement of Learning*, Bk II [iii, p. 419].

for an achievement, to have all the frailty of a human being and all the freedom from care of a god![41]

Here then is the heresy of the heathen: that a philosopher, by the discipline of his own mental efforts should so raise his human nature as to rival the condition of the gods. But the strange thing about Bacon's dismissal of Seneca is that the *Advancement* as a whole is dedicated to the proposition that the human mind is darkenened by a cloud of ignorance which can be removed by the discipline of the Baconian method, and that the entire condition of human life can be improved once the fruits of that method are applied. 'God hath framed the minde of man as a mirrour, or glasse, capable of the Image of the universall world, and joyful to receive the impression thereof.' Bacon's task was to revive and restore the mind's 'native and orginall motions (which by the strangenesse and darknesse of this Tabernacle of the bodie are sequestred)'.[42] The optimism of the heathen Seneca could not possibly be as alien to him as he pretended in the passage about the supreme good.

Bacon returned to Seneca's dictum in the *De Sapientia Veterum* of 1609, and this time he coupled it, as in the Adversity essay, with the legend of the voyage of Hercules. This is in the essay on Prometheus, the longest and most important of his interpretations of Greek myth.[43] Part of the fable tells how 'Hercules sailed across the ocean in a cup that was given him by the Sun, came to Caucasus, shot the eagle with his arrows, and set Prometheus free' (Spedding's translation).

41 I take this last sentence from the translation by Robin Campbell, in the Penguin Classics edition of Seneca's Letters, 1969, p. 103.

42 *Advancement of Learning*, Bk I [iii, pp. 265, 262] (Spedding reads 'notions', with 1629, for 1605's 'motions'.)

43 Works, vi, pp. 668–80. A facsimile of the 1609 text of *De Sapienta Veterum* together with the English translation by Sir Arthur Gorges, *The Wisedome of the Ancients*, 1619, was published by Garland, New York and London, 1976.

During the course of Bacon's interpretation of the fable, Prometheus is sometimes man's maker, sometimes man's benefactor, and sometimes man himself. One feature of the legend which particularly interested Bacon was the story that mankind was so ungrateful for the gift of fire which Prometheus had stolen from heaven that they brought an accusation to Jupiter against Prometheus and against fire, and that Jupiter rewarded them for their action. To explain this, Bacon divides mankind into two parts: those who are satisfied with human nature and its arts as they are, and those who are not content with them and rebel against them. Those who are satisfied, and keep admiring what mankind already possesses, are in fact the enemies of mankind. By supposing themselves perfect, they implicitly compare themselves with the gods, and in supposing that they have reached their limit, they have no interest in working to help their fellow men. Those on the other hand who arraign and accuse nature and the arts are stimulated to fresh industry and new discoveries (*nova inventa*). To prefer complaints against nature and the arts is pleasing to the gods, and draws down new benefits from the divine goodness.

The division of the human race into two kinds is repeated when Bacon considers another part of the fable, the gift of Pandora. There are the responsible people of the world, who are in the image of Prometheus, and there are the feckless followers of his brother Epimetheus, who improvidently take no care for the future and simply indulge themselves. Among the Prometheans, the assumption of forethought and responsibility exacts a heavy price, not only in the surrender of pleasures, but also in the cares, anxieties and fears which gnaw at them as the eagle gnawed at Prometheus' liver. Only a very few can free themselves from this constant perturbation, and they cannot attain this freedom by their innate qualities. They need help from outside. It is by the help of Hercules that they are able to achieve the fortitude and constancy of mind which is prepared for every fortune and can endure with patience.

It comes from beyond the ocean, it is received and brought to us from the Sun; for it comes of Wisdom, which is as the Sun, and of meditation upon the inconstancy and fluctuations of human life, which is as the navigation of the ocean.[44]

There is a great deal to think about here. That section of mankind who were the rebels against human nature and its arts are of course the same as the Prometheans, who suffer so greatly for their forethought and responsibility. By the help of Hercules these good people are able to withstand care and anxiety, and are able to fulfil the proper role of the human race (this is how I understand *ut providentiae commoda retinuerint*). They are able to navigate the ocean of the uncertainty of life. But what *is* this help which comes from afar? If it comes from outside man, comes indeed from the sun, nevertheless no divine source is named. It is wisdom and meditation which are able to navigate life's uncertainty. Bacon goes on to quote three lines from Virgil's *Georgics*, which he says join together wisdom and navigation.

Felix qui potuit rerum cognoscere causas,
Quique metus omnes et inexorabile fatum
Subiecit pedibus, strepitumque Acherontis avari.[45]

[Happy is he who learns the causes of things, and has cast beneath his feet all fears, and inexorable fate, and the clamour of greedy Acheron.]

It seems clear that this wisdom that comes from the sun, that brings fortitude and enables the best of men to continue with their work, is the same inspiration which led part of mankind to rebel against self-satisfaction and stimulated them to fresh industry and new discoveries. A remedy against doubt and

44 Works, vi, p. 675 (Spedding's translation).
45 *Georgics*, ii, 490–92.

despair which looks very like a Stoic achievement is in fact a
strikingly Baconian version of it, since the philosophy which it
is necessary to acquire is the new 'natural philosophy'—
knowledge of the causes of things. Bacon constantly abused
those who rely on ancient authority in investigating the world,
but here he is coolly invoking Seneca and Virgil in support of
the new science—always deviously and by implication, of
course. The navigation of life's uncertainy becomes one and
the same thing as the navigation of the ocean of thought for
'the reliefe of Mans estate'.[46] The fusion of the optimism of the
Stoic with the optimism of the scientist becomes clear as Bacon
continues after his citation of Virgil.

> Most elegantly it is added for the consolation and
> encouragement of men's minds, that that mighty hero
> sailed in a cup or pitcher; lest they should too much
> mistrust the narrowness and frailty of their own nature,
> or plead it in their own excuse, as though it were
> altogether incapable of this kind of fortitude and con-
> stancy: the true nature of which was well divined by
> Seneca, when he said, *It is true greatness to have in one
> the frailty of man and the security of a god.*

Bacon here cancels his rejection (in the *Advancement*) of
Seneca's confidence that we can triumph over the weakness of
human nature, but he accepts this confidence on his own
terms. What is especially powerful about Bacon's whole
discussion is that he has not simply substituted a scientific
remedy for a stoic remedy. He has absorbed Seneca's diagno-
sis—that the illness of mankind was unawareness of illness—
and he has absorbed the stoic remedy within the scientific
remedy. He still talks of unhappiness as the condition of life
for those who can think and can feel; he still talks of the need
to acquire fortitude and constancy of mind, and of navigating
the uncertainties of life, but fortitude for him includes the

---

46 *Advancement of Learning*, Bk I [iii, p. 294].

resolution to understand the causes of things and navigation includes the uncharted seas of knowledge.

As Bacon moves towards the conclusion of his Prometheus study, he starts to answer the obvious question, raised by his dismissal in the *Advancement* of Seneca's high claims for the potential of human nature on the grounds that Christianity disproved them. What has the acquisition of wisdom, brought from afar by Hercules, to do with the Christian faith? First, he interprets the legend of the attempt of Prometheus on the chastity of Minerva as a warning against trying to bring divine mystery under the dominion of sense and reason. Then he has the following conclusion.

> Such are the views which I conceive to be shadowed out in this so common and hacknied fable. It is true that there are not a few things beneath which have a wonderful correspondency with the mysteries of the Christian faith. The voyage of Hercules especially, sailing in a pitcher to set Prometheus free, seems to present an image of God the Word hastening in the frail vessel of the flesh to redeem the human race. But I purposely refrain myself from all licence of speculation of this kind, lest peradventure I bring strange fire to the altar of the Lord [*ne forte igne extraneo ad altare Domini utamur*].[47]

Here is a Promethean fire which would be going in the wrong direction: stolen from man and offered to God. The implication of the Minerva passage is that such offerings are refused. The christianization of Hercules remains a passing speculation.

To return then to the essay 'Of Adversitie'. We begin with another saying of Seneca, that the good things of prosperity are to be wished, but the good things of adversity are to be admired. And this is claimed not only to be 'an high speech' but higher than the other—the one about frailty and security.

47 Works, vi, p. 676.

Why should it be higher? The answer to this question explains the essay. We must expect that Bacon will try to treat this dictum as he treated the other: that is, incorporate it on his own terms.

The opposition between prosperity and adversity shadows the opposition between Epimetheus and Prometheus and the opposition between those who accept human nature and its arts and those who rebel against them. Adversity is the condition of life as it is recognized by sensitive and understanding people, and it is from adversity that all effort to improve the condition of life starts. The good things that belong to adversity are most certainly to be admired. At this time the word 'admire' had to do with wonder as much as approval. We would now say that these good things are more wonderful. The Latin word, given by Bacon, is 'mirabilia', a word whose meaning extended from the admirable to the miraculous. It is therefore only a slight jump to the word 'Miracles' in the next sentence. But the sentence as a whole is baffling. 'Certainly if Miracles, be the Commaund over Nature, they appeare most in Adversity.' Is Bacon referring to the miracles of Christ, which did indeed show command over nature, and were responses to adversity of various kinds? Then what could be the meaning of the conditional? The only way in which we can make sense of this sentence is to assume that Bacon still has in mind the marvels to be expected from scientific advance. 'If by "mirabilia" we are thinking of the miraculous benefits which command over nature will provide, they certainly derive from adversity.' Bacon's whole intellectual endeavour was directed to command over nature. We have already understood his contention that the urge to achieve this command can arise only from the Stoic's recognition of the misery of existence. Those finer souls who recognize adversity are impelled to rebel, and with the access of wisdom and meditation are stimulated to fresh industry and new discoveries, which will make man the master and not the slave of nature.

But now Bacon is suggesting the word 'miracles' for this mastery of nature. This does indeed bring strange fire to the altar of the Lord. Adversity, says the essay, is the blessing of the New Testament. These words confirm that by introducing the word 'miracles' into the second sentence of the essay, Bacon intended to bring into comparison the miracles of Christ with the amazing things performed by the scientist working to alleviate the adversity of human life. Adversity is the fallen state of mankind, from which Christ came to redeem us. To repeal the darkness of the fallen human mind was all along Bacon's explicit mission. The scientist treads in the footsteps of Christ and fulfils His mission.

This is certainly a very high speech of Seneca's, commending the good things produced in adversity, but its height is entirely Bacon's responsibility. When he says it is 'much too high for a Heathen', he admits his responsibility. These are levels which a heathen is not qualified to enter; but they are levels which Seneca did not in fact aspire to.

The parenthesis, '(much too high for a Heathen)', can, grammatically, refer backwards or forwards to either of the two sayings of Seneca, and, thematically, must refer to them both. The condescending treatment of the second Seneca dictum (the frailty of a man and the security of a god), treating it as another 'high' sentence, a 'transcendence' which would do better in poesy, is of course a blind. Bacon chooses disparagement as a tactical approach to allying the Seneca dictum with the legend of the Hercules voyage, even though he had already brought them together in an earlier published work. But the stakes are higher now, because the introduction of Christianity into the equation, so hesitant before, is now so prominent. The legend of Hercules sailing in a pitcher to rescue Prometheus 'seemeth not to be without mystery; Nay, and to have some approach, to the State of a Christian'. ('Mystery' here means an inner or secret meaning.) The interpretation is not now that which was tentatively suggested and then withdrawn at the end of the study in *Wisdom of the*

Ancients—that Hercules represented Christ incarnate in human flesh. Instead we have a much less mystical interpretation, that the legend provides a 'lively' description of Christian resolution, sailing in the frail bark of the flesh through the ocean of the world. The Hercules who brings relief to suffering mankind, and equips it with fortitude to bear and wisdom to advance, is not the incarnate Christ, but the altogether vaguer 'Christian resolution'.

On the one side, the Hercules legend is hooked to Seneca's saying; on the other side it is hooked to Christian resolution. Seneca is Christianized, as well as being made to speak in the cause of scientific advance. In this final treatment of the dictum, Bacon equates Seneca's *securitas*—the confidence of a god—with Christian resolution, just as he had equated Seneca's other statement, about the good things of adversity, with Christian promises. The voyage of Hercules becomes a Stoic voyage, a scientific voyage, and a Christian voyage. Scientific advance gets the blessing both of the ancients and Christianity. But it is a subdued kind of Christianity. In rejecting Hercules as Christ, Bacon is rejecting salvation through belief alone, through faith alone, through the sacraments alone. Human salvation is to come through knowledge and work. Hercules is the Christian driving force of the scientist, but he is not Christ.

Even so, Bacon recognizes that this coalescence of Seneca, the command over nature, and Christianity, however deviously it is put forward, is a very 'high' claim. 'But to speake in a Meane', he goes on. That is, he will now proceed in a more moderate or measured way. In fact, nothing that he says in the last third of the essay, though it is couched in much more conventional terms, is in dispute with what he has already written, and indeed the reference to the blessings of the New Testament enforces it.

Perhaps the ultimate importance of the essay, 'Of Adversitie', which seeks to sanctify Bacon's life-long philosophical programme with the authority of the ancients and of Christianity, is that Hercules, the hero who had set up his pillars to prevent the human mind from exploring uncharted waters, is now in command of the vessel which is sailing for the relief of man's estate.

CHAPTER EIGHT—MILTON
'That fatall and perfidious Bark'

The idea of the Fall is central in Milton's use of voyage imagery. *Lycidas* contains at the end a promise of hope or protection 'to all that wander in that perilous flood'—meaning all of fallen humanity. In discussing the poem, Isabel MacCaffrey pointed out the 'heavy change' from pastoral innocence to a dark journey by sea and an ultimately regained Paradise.[1] The idea of the Fall is most marked in apportioning the blame for the wrecking of Edward King's ship. Although the sea is named 'the remorseless deep', and 'that perilous flood', and although we have the vision of the 'sounding Seas' and 'the whelming tide' hurling the corpse 'beyond the stormy *Hebrides*' to 'the bottom of the monstrous world', it was not the violence of the sea nor the treachery of hidden rocks that caused the ship to sink.

> The Ayr was calm, and on the level brine,
> Sleek *Panope* with all her sisters play'd.
> It was that fatall and perfidious Bark
> Built in th' eclipse, and rigg'd with curses dark,
> That sunk so low that sacred head of thine.
>
> (98–102)[2]

The word 'sacred' has its Latin double sense of holy and accursed, consecrated and forfeit, participating in the divine and doomed to destruction. The language, wrote Brian Nellist, 'inevitably suggests metaphorical readings of the general fate attending man as fallen creature in the sea of this

1 MacCaffrey (1967), 26–28.
2 All quotations from Milton's verse are taken from the Clarendon Press text by Helen Darbishire, as given in the Oxford Standard Authors edition of 1958.

179

world'.[3] The heavenly spirit of man is betrayed and destroyed by the condition of fallen human life—what Bacon called 'the fraile Barke of the Flesh'. The 'eclipse' is no transient occlusion, but the withdrawal of heavenly light: we shall very shortly see the persistence of Milton's association of the sea-voyage with night-time. Sunlight is restored at the end of the poem (170) as Lycidas rises again like a new-dawning sun, 'through the dear might of him that walk'd the waves'.

Samson Agonistes also has its 'fatall and perfidious Bark'—Dalila, of course, in the renowned simile of the Chorus.

> But who is this, what thing of Sea or Land?
> Femal of sex it seems,
> That so bedeckt, ornate, and gay,
> Comes this way sailing
> Like a stately Ship
> Of *Tarsus*, bound for th' Iles
> Of *Javan* or *Gadier*
> With all her bravery on, and tackle trim,
> Sails filld, and streamers waving,
> Courted by all the winds that hold them play . . .
>
>   (710–19)

Samson trusted himself to Dalila, and she betrayed him. But in spite of this very significant image of the treacherous beauty of a stately ship, Dalila is not the most important of the ships in *Samson Agonistes*. The wrecked vessel which is the subject of the poem is Samson's own life.

> How could I once look up, or heave the head,
> Who like a foolish Pilot have shipwrackt
> My Vessel trusted to me from above,
> Gloriously riggd . . . ?
>
>   (197–200)

The Chorus picture Dalila as the helmsman of this vessel.

---

3 Nellist (1974), p. 206.

> What Pilot so expert but needs must wreck
> Imbarkt with such a Stears-mate at the Helm?
> (1044–45)

God put his trust in Samson, who betrayed Him by putting his trust in Dalila, who betrayed *him*. The idea of the perfidious barque is heavily qualified by the overriding reponsibility of the pilot, so that Dalila, as ship or helmsman, has only a secondary responsibility. This may seem a dramatic alteration of what is told in *Lycidas*, but of course it is only a change of emphasis or perspective. Individual responsibility is not the focus of *Lycidas*; the focus is rather the condition of fallen humanity, of which Edward King was a victim. How far the victim collaborates in his own destruction is the focus of the later poem.[4]

In *Paradise Lost* the seafarer is constantly used as an emblem of the benighted condition of fallen humanity. In Book V God sends Raphael to warn Adam of his imminent danger. Raphael flies to the gate of Heaven for his long descent through space.

> From hence, no cloud, or, to obstruct his sight,
> Starr interpos'd, however small he sees,
> Not unconform to other shining Globes,
> Earth and the Gard'n of God, with Cedars crownd
> Above all Hills. As when by night the Glass
> Of *Galileo*, less assur'd, observes
> Imagind Lands and Regions in the Moon:
> Or Pilot from amidst the *Cyclades*
> *Delos* or *Samos* first appeering kenns
> A cloudy spot. Down thither prone in flight
> He speeds, and through the vast Ethereal Skie
> Sailes between worlds and worlds . . .
> (V. 257–68)

This is a very difficult passage, and Thomas Greene has engagingly suggested that the uncertainty of the reader 'peer-

4 For an extended analysis of the sea imagery in *Samson*, see Lewalski.

ing to make out the construction', mirrors the uncertainty of the pilot.[5] However we read the first sentence, it is obvious that the piercing angelic vision of Raphael can pick out Earth from among a myriad bodies in space and he can make his way directly to it. In contrast, the great Galileo, with the most advanced optical instrument, can only make out what he thinks are countries in the moon. And then the pilot. Commentators point out that Samos was not one of the Cyclades, as though Milton had made a mistake. It would be crucial for the poet *not* to make a mistake here. The pilot is making his way among the Cyclades, and there appears before him something that might be Delos or it might be Samos—eighty miles away. He can't tell: it's only a blur, a 'cloudy spot'. The word 'kens' is important; it is frequently used by Milton, and while 'observe' or 'descry' will usually serve as a synonym, both these words suggest a perfect relationship between what is seen and what is really there. In fact, imperfect vision, imperfect knowledge, and imperfect navigation will constantly drive the mariner to a false recognition of what he sees. It is better to translate 'ken' as 'make out'. Galileo sees what possibly might be land; the pilot sees real land, but cannot identify it. Milton introduces his comparison between Raphael and the fallen astronomer and pilot with the words 'As when'. What he really means is 'It was not at all as when . . .'

All this would seem to be a cumbersome way of making an obvious point—that fallen mankind can't see as well as angels can. Milton's purpose in contrasting the keen vision and assured flight of Raphael with the uncertain probing of Galileo's telescope and the faltering perceptions of a seafarer seems to be ironic. Raphael is making his journey to warn man to beware falling. It is a journey in vain; Milton's similes tell us he need not have bothered. Just the same ironic technique has

5 Greene, p. 385. There is a good analysis of the syntax in MacCaffrey (1975), 22–23.

already been used in describing Uriel's descent in Book IV to
warn Gabriel that 'one of the banisht crew' is at large.

> Thither came *Uriel*, gliding though the Eeven
> On a Sun beam, swift as a shooting Starr
> In *Autumn* thwarts the night, when vapors fir'd
> Impress the Air, and shews the Mariner
> From what point of his Compass to beware
> Impetuous winds . . .
>
> (IV. 555–60)

A seaman struggling at night to avoid the antagonism of
natural forces is a potent representative of benighted, afflicted
mankind. Even as Uriel comes to warn Gabriel to watch out
for Satan, Milton grimly reminds us of the uselessness of their
endeavours.

The first of these similes (all of them inappropriate or
awkward as regards any real similitude), by which a seaman in
difficulties at night serves to inject a reminder of the Fall, is the
early comparison of Satan, prone in the fiery flood of Hell, to
the huge sea-beast Leviathan (I. 200–10). 'The Pilot of some
small night-founderd Skiff', deceived into thinking the monster is an island that will protect him,

> Moors by his side under the Lee, while Night
> Invests the Sea, and wished Morn delayes.

Stevie Davies rightly points out that the thrust of this passage
is not to warn against the danger of trusting to false appear-
ances but to make the reader share the helplessness and anxiety
of the diminutive seaman. 'The feeling of the passage, with its
extraordinary atmosphere of foreboding, the slowing-down
of time through the vigilance of anxiety ('wished Morn
delayes'), and the strangeness of the dark, illimitable landscape, is surely of the order "There, but for the grace of God,
go I".'[6] The most powerful and moving of these sea images is

6 Davies, 122.

that which follows the speech of Mammon, advising the fallen
angels to accept their situation.

> He scarce had finisht, when such murmur filld
> Th' Assembly, as when hollow Rocks retain
> The sound of blustring winds, which all night long
> Had rous'd the Sea, now with hoarse cadence lull
> Sea-faring men orewatcht, whose Bark by chance
> Or Pinnace anchors in a craggy Bay
> After the Tempest; Such applause was heard
> As *Mammon* ended, and his Sentence pleas'd,
> Advising peace.
>
> (II. 284–92)

In this complex image the fallen angels are first the noise of the
wind—only a quiet and sleepy echo of the din of their
tempestuous rebellion; but they are also the exhausted mariners, longing for rest however threatening their situation may
be, lulled to sleep by the very same winds which have attacked
them. These mariners whom the fallen angels resemble are
none but ourselves, worn-out travellers afflicted by the 'snow
and haile and stormie gust and flaw' which were an immediate
result of the disobedience of Adam and Eve (X. 698).
Perilously anchored in a craggy bay, all we want is rest.

This splendid image anticipates and summarizes the poem
to come. What rouses the fallen angels from their torpor is the
heroism and self-sacrifice of Satan. What saves them destroys
us, reduces us to the level which makes the simile possible. To
rouse us from our torpor, then, an act of heroism and self-
sacrifice will also be required, and will be provided by the Son
of God.

Once Satan has done his work, Sin and Death start building
a bridge or causeway from Hell to Earth through Chaos.

> Then Both from out Hell Gates into the waste
> Wide Anarchie of *Chaos* damp and dark
> Flew divers, and with power (thir power was great)

Hovering upon the Waters, what they met
Solid or slimie, as in raging Sea
Tost up and down, together crowded drove
From each side shoaling towards the mouth of Hell.
As when two Polar Winds blowing adverse
Upon the *Cronian* Sea, together drive
Mountains of Ice, that stop th' imagind way
Beyond *Petsora* Eastward, to the rich
Cathaian Coast.

(X. 282–93)

So a pathway is created to facilitate the passage of devils to Earth and people to Hell. And the piling up of the aggregated sludge of Chaos is compared to the work of the winds in piling up icebergs to stop the passage of explorers trying to find the North-East Passage through the Arctic to the riches of Cathay. Here is another failure of correspondence in a simile, which this time is not to be resolved by reading 'not at all as when' for 'as when'. In reading through Hakluyt and Purchas for his history of Muscovia (see p. 187), Milton would have come across Henry Hudson's failure, in both 1607 and 1608, on his mission for the Muscovy Company 'to discover a passage by the North Pole to Japan and China'.[7] Each time he was halted by ice. He then turned from the North-East to the North-West Passage, and in 1611 he was trapped in the ice in Hudson Bay, where he died. This thirst to find an easy route to the riches of the east is the key to the simile, emphasizing as it does the longing of fallen mankind for unattainable compensations. That which blocks the mariners' covetous way to their objective has a very odd resemblance to the path to hell. They do not reach their materialist paradise; they may be on their way to hell instead.

That travel, and sea-travel especially, is literally and metaphorically the activity of fallen humanity is a concept of great

7 Edwards (1988), p. 125.

antiquity and long durance. It was a standard feature of
descriptions of the Golden Age that in that initial period of
innocence there was no *need* to travel.[8] People were content to
stay on their own ground and enjoy what the earth yielded in
abundance. Mortals knew no shores except their own, as Ovid
put it in the *Metamorphoses*. This is the condition aspired to at
the end of Book II of Virgil's *Georgics*, when others are left to
'vex with oars the perilous seas', and it is seen as the
characteristic of one who has murdered his brother to 'seek a
fatherland that lies beneath another sun'. Voyaging came in
with the corruption and avarice of the Iron Age. Innocence
and Travel are contradictions in terms. So it is not really a
surprise that Milton should view the ocean way to Cathay as
resembling the causeway to Hell, or that he should persist in
similes in which Satan is brought into comparison with
mariners voyaging in search of wealth or new territories.
These similes, because of the great beauty of their sea-pictures,
remain a great puzzle, though it is now generally accepted that
they are part of an extended critique that sees exploration,
oversea trade, and colonization as activities belonging to a race
fallen under a curse brought about by the voyage of Satan to
the newly created Earth.[9]

> Mean while the Adversary of God and Man,
> *Satan* with thoughts inflam'd of highest design,
> Puts on swift wings, and toward the Gates of Hell
> Explores his solitary flight; som times
> He scours the right hand coast, som times the left,
> Now shaves with level wing the Deep, then soares
> Up to the fiery Concave touring high.
> As when farr off at Sea a Fleet descri'd
> Hangs in the Clouds, by *Æquinoctial* Winds
> Close sailing from *Bengala*, or the Iles
> Of *Ternate* and *Tidore*, whence Merchants bring

8 See the evidence collected by Lovejoy and Boas, *passim*.
9 See for example Evans, pp. 46–47 and Quint, pp. 194–95.

Thir spicie Drugs: they on the Trading Flood
Through the wide *Ethiopian* to the Cape
Ply stemming nightly toward the Pole. So seemd
Farr off the flying Fiend . . .

(II. 629–43)

Yet another night-time voyage. Perhaps this beautiful evocation of maritime enterprise (like others) had its origin in the
ideas of the thirty-year-old poet (admirer of Ralegh[10]) for a
national epic, centred on the 'high-hearted heroes' of the
Arthurian round table.[11] If so, Milton's attitude to these later
heroes of the deep had changed by the time he was forty, and
was combing though the voyages collected by Hakluyt and
Purchas for his notes towards a history of Russia, published
after his death as *A Brief History of Moscovia*.[12] Chapter Five,
relating the English voyages of discovery of the mid-sixteenth
century, begins as follows.

> The discovery of *Russia* by the northern Ocean, made
> first, of any Nation that we know, by *English* men, might
> have seem'd an enterprise almost heroick; if any higher
> end than the excessive love of Gain and Traffick, had
> animated the design.

However, because 'good events ofttimes arise from evil
occasions', he will tell the story of 'this adventurous Voiage'.[13]
That Satan's flight to Earth should regularly be compared
with the efforts of indefatigable explorers and traders on the
high seas certainly questions the motives and morals of the
sea-adventurers. But the full implications of the similes are
complex, intricate, and mobile.

10 Hill, p. 61.
11 *Mansus*, lines 80–84.
12 For the date, occasion, and intention of this work, see G. B. Parkes'
introduction to the Yale edition of Milton's prose works, viii, pp. 454–72.
13 *Complete Prose Works of John Milton*, Yale University Press, Vol.
viii, p. 524.

   In her outstanding chapter, 'Satan's Voyage',[14] Isabel Mac-
Caffrey compared Satan's flight to Earth with the 'dark
voyage' of all quest-literature. This dark voyage thus becomes
the sign of the first fallen being. Milton associates Satan with
questing heroes such as the Argonauts and Ulysses, noting
that this heroism is wholly irrelevant to the life of Heaven or
Paradise, where there is no aching search for reward and rest.
Satan's quest is linked with our own fate as voyagers through
the unknown. MacCaffrey shows the fallen angels as wan-
derers, too, the 'dark and drearie Vale' through which 'th'
adventrous Bands' travel (II. 614–21) being the allegorical vale
of tears through which all people must pass.
   MacCaffrey was chiefly concerned with voyage as myth
rather than the specific voyaging of Milton's age, but she
noted that 'Milton's geographical interests' inspired his representation of Satan's journey (p. 201). It seems certain that
Milton's reading in Hakluyt and Purchas, and not only the
Russian voyages, provided the scenery for the wanderings of
both Satan and his fellows, 'on bold adventure to discover
wide / That dismal World' (II. 571–72). They find 'a frozen
Continent / . . . dark and wilde, beat with perpetual storms'
(587–88). In order to make real the spiritual plight of the fallen
angels, Milton had recourse to the published accounts of
Arctic voyages. And because of the reciprocity of his similitudes, these voyages take on the darkness of the primary fall.

                                                I abroad
      Through all the coasts of dark destruction seek
      Deliverance for us all.

                                            (II. 463–65)

Thus Satan. And this is basically the battle-cry of the European adventurer seeking to enlarge the territories of his
homeland. Trade, living-space, gold, and power may not seem
to fall under the heading of 'deliverance', but all oversea

14 MacCaffrey (1967), pp. 179–206.

enterprise started from discontent with what one had, from the desire to change and improve one's condition. The fallen angels, searching to find 'if any Clime perhaps / Might yeild them easier habitation' (572–73), are not in a wholly different position from the intending settlers who went out from England with fleet after fleet from Elizabethan times onwards. If it is trade rather than settlement, still it is something to enhance the conditions of life that is sought. The 'spicie Drugs' brought back from '*Ternate* and *Tidore*' are not narcotics, but exotic medicaments with the seductive promise of enhancing life. In their small way they follow the promise of Eve's apple. As Satan gets through the worst of his journey through Chaos, and nears 'this pendant World', Milton compares him with 'a weather-beat'n Vessel' which 'holds / Gladly the Port, though Shrouds and Tackle torn'. This vessel is 'full-fraught with mischievous revenge'; by implication, every trading ship returning from the East after a difficult passage brings with it satanic temptation. 'His journies end and our beginning woe' (III. 633).

The equation of Satan's voyage to Earth with colonizing enterprise is clear enough. Beelzebub, speaking on Satan's behalf (II. 379–80), suggests the mission to Earth, speaking of it as 'this new World' and 'the happy Ile' (403, 410). It will involve a 'dreadful voyage'. The plan is to destroy this new part of God's empire,

> or possess
> All as our own, and drive as wee were driven,
> The punie habitants, or if not drive,
> Seduce them to our Party . . .
> (II. 365–68)

After Satan's conquest, Adam and Eve are specifically compared to the American natives whom '*Columbus* found' (IX. 1115–18).

David Armitage has brought forward strong arguments that in his anti-imperial stance Milton was particularly moved by

Cromwell's expansionist policies, particularly towards the West Indies, which he thought endangered the ideal of a republic.[15] In the controversy aroused by the failure of the expeditionary force under Venables against Hispaniola much had been made of Spanish cruelty towards the inhabitants of the West Indies (one of the traditional justifications for English interference). Armitage shows that Milton was led to oppose colonialism as a whole, whichever country directed it.

A parallel between Satan's attack on Adam and Eve and the despoliation by European nations of the oversea territories they came to occupy is contained in the most moving of all these voyage images. Satan is drawing near to Paradise.

> Now gentle gales
> Fanning thir odoriferous wings dispense
> Native perfumes, and whisper whence they stole
> Those balmie spoiles. As when to them who saile
> Beyond the *Cape of Hope*, and now are past
> *Mozambic*, off at Sea North-East windes blow
> *Sabean* Odours from the spicie shoare
> Of *Arabie* the blest, with such delay
> Well pleas'd they slack thir course, and many a League
> Cheard with the grateful smell old Ocean smiles.
> So entertaind those odorous sweets the Fiend
> Who came thir bane . . .
>
> (IV. 156–67)

For once, 'as when' seems to mean 'as when'. The intoxicating perfumes from the spicy shore of Araby the blest typify the seductiveness of every oversea earthly paradise, Virginia, Guiana, Tahiti, for the European voyagers 'who came thir bane'. So Drayton encouraged the English colonists:

15 'John Milton: poet against empire' in *Milton and Republicanism*, ed. D. Armitage, A. Himy and Q. Skinner, Cambridge 1995, pp. 206–25; and D. Armitage, *The British Empire and the Civic Tradition*, Cambridge PhD, 1991.

When as the Lushious smell
Of that delicious Land,
Above the Seas that flowes,
The cleere Wind throwes,
Your Hearts to swell
Approching the deere Strand . . .[16]

The whole sad history of the West Indian islands, and, in the century following Milton's death, the Pacific islands, is indicated as a repetition of Satan's assault on the innocence of Adam and Eve.

The similitudes between Satan and the seafarer conclude with the perplexing comparison of Satan as serpent, wriggling his way towards Eve, and a ship gaining its objective by tacking.

               With tract oblique
At first, as one who sought access, but feard
To interrupt, side-long he works his way.
As when a Ship by skilful Stearsman wrought
Nigh Rivers mouth or Foreland, where the Wind
Veres oft, as oft so steers, and shifts her Saile;
So varied hee, and of his tortuous Traine
Curld many a wanton wreath in sight of *Eve*,
To lure her Eye . . .   (IX. 510–18)

Both Satan and the pilot gain their objectives by a devious indirect route. But the moral conjunction, by which the skill of the pilot is compared to the cunning guile of Satan, seems very unfair. Is it satanic to manoeuvre a boat successfully? Has the idea of travel by sea as a fallen occupation, especially in its objectives of trade and imperialism, as a restless occupation opposed to the stillness and peace of innocence and bliss, so absorbed Milton that its every function, even adjusting sails to the wind, becomes a sinister activity? There is something

16 'Ode to the Virginian Voyage', *Works*, ed. Hebel, 1932, ii, p. 364.

stubbornly resistant in that skilful steersman, which makes us wonder if in some way, as with Raphael and the Pilot, the principle of 'as-when-equals-not-as-when' applies in the comparison.

The picture of the pilot, skilfully accommodating his ship to the fitful and unpredictable winds, is of deep significance. A number of commentators have pointed out that it was only a chance turbulence in the elements that enabled Satan to make his voyage to Earth at all.

> Fluttring his pennons vain plumb down he drops
> Ten thousand fadom deep, and to this hour
> Down had been falling, had not by ill chance
> The strong rebuff of som tumultuous cloud
> Instinct with Fire and Nitre hurried him
> As many miles aloft.
>
> (II. 933–38)

'The fate of mankind is made to depend on this random buffet of a cloud in Chaos,' wrote F. T. Prince.[17] Satan's success, it is made clear at several points, depends on good luck, and making the best use of the circumstances which he finds.[18] Man as voyager by sea is the best possible representation of the way the fallen human race is forced to imitate the condition of the being who caused its fall. The voyager by sea is at the mercy of the elements and dependent for any progress on his skill in making the most of what offers. It is the sea more than the winds to which Milton gives the role of representing the world of circumstance and contingency within which humanity is forced to work. In *Lycidas* the sea was the remorseless deep and the perilous flood. In *Paradise Lost*, it is the wildness of the ocean which makes it the fittest metaphor for the state of

17 In his edition of *Paradise Lost*, Bks I and II, Oxford University Press, 1962, p. 169.
18 Alastair Fowler, in his note on this passage, compares IV. 530, IX. 85, 421, 423.

Chaos—that 'vast and boundless Deep', 'a dark, / Illimitable Ocean without bound' (I. 177, II. 891–92). Satan describes how he has 'Voyag'd th' unreal, vast, unbounded Deep / Of horrible confusion' (X. 471–72). At the time of Creation, the King of Glory surveys Chaos, 'outrageous as a Sea, dark, wasteful, wilde' (VII. 212). In a complex and detailed narrative in Book VII, following the biblical account, Milton describes how the real ocean was created out of the metaphoric ocean of Chaos—'the great receptacle / Of congregated Waters he calld Seas' (307–08). After the Fall, these bound-in seas returned to something like the wild state they originated in, as the loosened fury of the winds afflicted them (X. 692–706), and this tumult and turbulence is the life which mankind must journey through.

The best symbol of our benighted condition is the voyage through turbulent seas. The best examples of our benighted condition are voyages—actual voyages, undertaken to acquire territory or riches. Our boldest endeavours are tainted by the corruption that Satan foisted on to us. It is the purpose of the *Paradise Lost* similes to condemn our proud maritime adventures as products of the Fall, and to enlarge those maritime adventures into symbols of the fallen condition. Satan has ruined us, and we have become like him. If, however, these similes declare that we are like Satan, they also declare that Satan is like us. Or, if that is impossible, then, by the application of the 'not-as-when' principle, that he is *not* like us. These similes never congeal into simple equivalence, but remain effervescent, capable at different times and in different lights of suggesting both an idea and its opposite.

There is not one of them that does not in some sort and to some extent evoke admiration and pity for the seafarers. These sailing ships in their missions in far-off seas are beautiful, and courage and skill are needed to bring them safely through. The men in them may be lost souls engaged on unworthy enterprises; but they are also victims of higher powers, struggling with every nerve to survive. Satan is the first created being

impelled to travel, and by means of the voyage similes, some
of the initiative, daring, skill, persistence and endurance of the
explorers by sea is reflected back on him. That much is easy to
grant. It was long the argument of those who would not accept
that Milton was of the devil's party without knowing it that
there had to be grandeur in the adversary of God and man, and
that the extent of his fall had to be seen in the ruined remains of
his nobility. Satan is elevated by his kinship with the seafarers
whose enterprises are simultaneously debased.

Are we able also to grant to Satan the sympathy and pity
which we feel so often for the voyagers in the similes? As
Isabel MacCaffrey argued, the plight of Satan and the fallen
angels foreshadows the human predicament of displacement
and weary search. In the great image given to the murmur of
the assembly (II. 284–92; see above p. 184) the fallen angels are
linked with 'Sea-faring men orewatcht', sharing our longing
for rest even in times of great danger. But that sympathy may
well be a trap for the reader. We need to go back to the voyage-
simile at the end of Book II, as Satan's journey through Chaos
draws to an end.

> But now at last the sacred influence
> Of light appears, and from the walls of Heav'n
> Shoots farr into the bosom of dim Night
> A glimmering dawn; here Nature first begins
> Her fardest verge, and *Chaos* to retire
> As from her outmost works a brok'n foe
> With tumult less and with less hostil din,
> That *Satan* with less toil, and now with ease
> Wafts on the calmer wave by dubious light,
> And like a weather-beat'n Vessel holds
> Gladly the Port, though Shrouds and Tackle torn;
> Or in the emptier waste, resembling Air,
> Weighs his spred wings, at leasure to behold
> Farr off th' Empyreal Heav'n, extended wide
> In circuit, undetermind square or round,

With Opal Towrs and Battlements adornd
Of living Saphire, once his native Seat;
And fast by hanging in a gold'n Chain
This pendant World, in bigness as a Starr
Of smallest Magnitude close by the Moon.
Thither full fraught with mischievous revenge,
Accurst, and in a cursed hour he hies.

(1034–55)

The brief comparison of Satan's arrival at his journey's end with a ship reaching harbour after a difficult voyage takes us back to the extended opening comparison with the trading fleet at night (see pp. 186–87). It therefore plays an important part in identifying Satan's mission with human voyaging and the devaluing of it—especially in the suggestion of the damage latent in the cargo. But the link works the other way too, in conveying the exhausting difficulty of what Satan had undertaken. How far do we go in our sympathy?

That the weather-beaten vessel gladly *holds* the port seems important. The synonyms of commentators—'makes for', 'reaches', even 'remains in'—fail to register the sense of the enfeebled mariners tenaciously keeping course as they bring their stricken ship into harbour. What is unwritten in these two lines seems a powerful repudiation of Satan in favour of the human mariners. They are coming home perhaps; at any rate their pleasure and relief is not only for the end of their sufferings but for the welcome they expect. Satan on the other hand is returning to regions which were 'once his native Seat', from which he has been banished because of his rebellion, and he can look forward to no welcome whatsoever.

Both the tenor and the vehicle of this comparison keep feeding and qualifying each other. Satan's influence undermines man's regard for the heroism of travel and the value of its rewards. Man's influence suggests the initiative, courage, skill and endurance of Satan. But there comes a moment of disjunction, when the two arms of the comparison seem to push each other away, and a human sympathy evoked by the voyage simile will not transfer to Satan, distinguishing him as foreign to us, worse than us. This sense of disjunction, of repudiation, is surely present too in the simile of Satan making his way towards Eve like a skilful steersman bringing his ship round a foreland or into a river. I have suggested that this comparison is central, in that it places fallen mankind (the victim) in the same condition as Satan (the aggressor), forced to contrive an existence by battling with chance and adversity. The struggle of the mariner with wind and tide is the perfect emblem of the shared condition. But as the aggressor and the victim move together, they move apart. It's not just vanity to refuse the identification of the wily archfiend deceiving Eve with a seaman making his way home. There is more than one order of deviousness. Spontaneous indignation on behalf of the sailor may in part be a sign of human weakness, but there is a difference between those who can be saved and those who cannot. Human values are not always dragged down in the similes in which Satan is a voyager.

In Book X of *Paradise Lost*, Milton told of Satan's return to Hell to give a triumphant account of how he had 'Voyag'd th' unreal, vast, unbounded Deep' to find the 'new created World', how he had corrupted the inhabitants and made them the prey of Sin and Death. He was rewarded with the 'universal hiss' of his myriad supporters, all turned into 'complicated monsters', and was himself transformed into a serpent. For mankind there are different possibilities. Following the biblical account, Milton created another ocean, the waters above the firmament, 'the clear *Hyaline*, the Glassie Sea' (VII. 619). In a wonderful passage in Book III, Milton described how those who have, as it were, survived the Fall by resisting Satan make their voyage to the gate of Heaven.

> Underneath a bright Sea flowd
> Of Jasper, or of liquid Pearle, whereon
> Who after came from Earth, sailing arriv'd,

Wafted by Angels, or flew ore the Lake
Rapt in a Chariot drawn by fiery Steeds.
(III. 518–22)

This serene voyage, in the light, and untroubled by the violence of the elements, is the 'large recompense' offered to Lycidas, and 'to all that wander in that perilous flood'.

CONCLUSION

The period which takes us from *The Faerie Queene* to *Paradise Lost* marks a critical stage in a centuries-long argument on the moral status of exploration and travel. In writing on Milton I spoke of the customary association of the beginning of travel with the end of the Age of Gold. Anxiety about the motive for travel persisted well into the Enlightenment, and can be found not only in Rousseau and Diderot[1] but also in George Forster, the brilliant young scientist who went round the world with Cook on his second voyage.[2] In *The Enchafed Flood* (1951) W. H. Auden contrasted the earlier period, in which suspicion of the sea prevailed and the image for normal society was the City or the Garden, with the Romantic period. The distinctive new notes of the Romantic attitude, he wrote, were as follows.

> (1) To leave the land and the city is the desire of every man of sensibility and honour.
> (2) The sea is the real situation and the voyage is the true condition of man. (p. 23)

It is a long time before we reach the stage when the voyage is the true condition of man, and we also find that the seeds of the divided mind, which is so apparent in some of the writers we have been examining, were implanted early.

For those who study the travel debate,[3] the standard anti-travel *locus* in classical times is the renowned chorus in Seneca's *Medea* (301–79) in which, lamenting the trouble caused to Corinth by Jason's arrival with Medea, the Chorus deplore the whole business of voyaging, and the restlessness

---

1 See Pagden, esp. pp. 157–58.
2 Edwards (1994), pp. 115–22.
3 E.g., Gillies, pp. 19–25.

which sent the Argo out in search of the Golden Fleece, which
led to Jason's marriage.

> quod fuit huius
> pretium cursus? aurea pellis
> maiusque mari Medea malum,
> merces prima digna carina.
> (361–63)[4]

[Of this voyage what was the prize? The golden fleece—
and Medea, worse evil than the sea, worthy to be the first
ship's merchandise.]

Here is the *damnosa hereditas* of voyaging: the boon and the
curse inextricably mixed. The main worry of the Chorus
about voyaging in general is that it has erased the established
boundaries by means of which one's identity is established.
We know who we are because of where we are. But now that
sea-travel is the norm, all boundaries have gone. Then comes
the astonishing prophecy of discovery of new worlds.

> Venient annis saecula seris,
> quibus Oceanus vincula rerum
> laxet et ingens pateat tellus
> Tethysque novos detegat orbes
> nec sit terris ultima Thule.
> (375–79)

[There will come an age in the far-off years when Ocean
shall unloose the bonds of things, when the whole broad
earth shall be revealed, when Tethys shall disclose new
worlds and Thule not be the limit of the lands.]

It is hard to think back to a time when you were pretty certain
that there were unknown lands and unknown peoples somewhere upon the earth, and you hadn't the least desire to know
more about them—indeed you feared the opening up of the

---

4 Text and translation from the Loeb edition.

world, since it involved the continuance of the dissolving of boundaries, which was already challenging the distinctiveness of one's identity.[5] It seems like the fear of spring among the shrivelled souls of Eliot's *The Waste Land*. But there is a real ambiguity in these lines. The Chorus are concerned, like most characters in Seneca's plays, to protect themselves against the raw edges of unpalatable circumstance by weaving convenient explanations.[6] And they say that the trouble is that Medea is a foreigner, and she wouldn't be here causing difficulty if it were not for all this new-fangled ocean-travel. We should not ask Seneca, with his radical and sceptical intelligence, to believe everything his characters say. The poetry moves against the Chorus in the last lines of their speech, and the sense of awe at the revealing one day in the future of the concealed world may contain fear but it is not limited to fear. Indeed, throughout the chorus, there is the feeling that those who cling to the familiarity of ignorance are not necessarily the best of mortals. I think that the reciprocal thrust of attraction and repulsion, or welcome and rejection, which is so marked in the long debate on the opening of new horizons, is certainly present in the *locus classicus* of opposition to voyaging, Seneca's *Medea* chorus.

It is very interesting that the same procedure, of giving the case against voyaging to a speaker who does not necessarily speak for the author, was adopted by Albinovanus Pedo, in the remarkable fragment of his epic on the expeditions of Germanicus, which is all that survives of his work, preserved as a quotation in a *suasoria* of Seneca the Elder. Germanicus pushes out from the Ems into the North Sea, and his fleet is shattered by a tremendous storm. The poet describes them as exiles from the known territories of the world, travelling

---

5 For an absorbing account of the primeval fear of the loss of boundaries, see Gillies, especially Chapter 1, 'Mapping the Other'. Auden adduces Horace, *Odes*, I, iii, which is certainly relevant, though it is a playful expression of the impiety of crossing boundaries.

6 See Edwards (1990), p. 123.

though darkness towards the very edge of nature. But he gives
it to a common sailor on the prow of his ship, straining his
eyes to see what lies ahead, to moralise on their situation.

> quo ferimur? fugit ipse dies orbemque relictum
> ultima perpetuis claudit natura tenebris.
> anne alio positas ultra sub cardine gentes
> atque alium flabris intactum quaerimus orbem?
> di revocant rerumque vetant cognoscere finem
> mortales oculos: aliena quid aequora remis
> et sacras violamus aquas divumque quietas
> turbamus sedes?[7]

[Where are we being taken? Day itself is fleeing, and
nature, at her furthest point, encloses the world we have
left in perpetual darkness. Are we seeking races elsewhere, beneath another pole, another world where no
wind blows? The gods are calling us back and forbid us to
perceive with mortal eyes the boundary of nature. Why
do we violate with our oars these seas belonging to
others, these sacred waters? Why disturb the quiet abode
of the gods?]

This is strong stuff, and it is about as far as we can go in
condemning the rash impiety of venturing by sea. In his
account of the development of the human race in Book V of
De rerum natura, Lucretius remarks that in earliest times 'the
wicked art of navigation lay concealed' (*improba navigii ratio
tum caeca iacebat*),[8] but there are no raptures about the state of
primitive ignorance, and the later account of the development
of the arts of mankind places navigation along with agriculture, law, and poetry as part of the progress of mankind.

> Namque alid ex alio clarescere et ordine debet
> artibus, ad summum donec venere cacumen.

---

7 *Suasoria prima*. Text from edition by H. J. Müller, 1887, reprinted
1963, p. 530.
8 Lovejoy and Boas, pp. 227–28.

[Things must be brought to light one after another and in
due order in the arts, until they have reached their highest
point.][9]

This proto-Baconian stance is repeated by Manilius in his
work on astronomy in the first century AD. Primitive times
are not praised for their simplicity but scorned for their
unenquiring torpor; 'each thought he knew enough'. Men did
not dare trust their lives to the waves. But in more enlightened
times, when long ages had sharpened human minds, 'the
wandering sailor penetrated hidden seas, and the ship made
trade with unknown lands' (*vagus in caecum penetravit navita
pontum, / fecit et ignotis linter commercia terris*).[10]

It was with Dante's implacable treatment of Ulysses in the
Inferno that the Pillars of Hercules (the Straits of Gibraltar)
became the great ambiguous symbol of the ethics of voyaging.
To go through them, is it a birth or a death? As no ancient
writer had given an account of the last days of Ulysses, Dante
provided one. His Ulysses has no interest in returning home;
he longs to keep on voyaging, to find out more about the
world.

> Io e' compagni eravam vecchi e tardi
> quando venimmo a quella foce stretta
> dov' Ercule segnò li suoi riguardi
>
> acciò che l' uom più oltre non si metta.
>   (XXVI, 106–09)[11]

[I and my companions were old and slow when we came
to that narrow passage where Hercules set his markers, so
that man should pass no further.]

Ulysses encourages his men as they venture into the unknown.
'You were not made to live like brutes, but to pursue virtue

9 Text and translation from Lovejoy and Boas, pp. 236–37.
10 *Ibid.*, pp. 376–77.
11 Text from G. Petrocchi, 1966.

and knowledge.' They see an immensely high mountain, but as they see it a violent tempest arises, and their vessel is sucked under the waves—'as pleased Another' (*com' altrui piacque*). So Ulysses is punished for his temerity and hardihood in pushing out into the open seas to find out more about the world.

Dante was taken on directly by Tasso—writing 350 years later. David Quint has stressed the importance of the boat journey by Carlo and Rinaldo in Book XV of *Gierusalemme Liberata* (completed in 1575 and published 1580–81).[12] As they come to the Straits of Gibraltar, their guide, Fortune, describes how Hercules, who dared not assay the ocean main, set up his pillars. Here is Fairfax's 1600 translation.

> Within his pillours would he have impaild
> The overdaring wit of mankinde vaine;
>   Till Lord *Ulysses* did those bounders pas,
>   To see and know he so desirous was;
>
> He past those pillours, and in open wave
> ¨ Of the broad sea first his bould sailes untwind;
>   But yet the greedie Ocean was his grave . . .

But many peoples live beyond the Pillars, and in time their lands will be discovered and they will learn the Christian gospel.

> Thy ship (*Columbus*) shall her canvasse wing
> Spread ore that world, that yet concealed lies,
> That scant swift fame her lookes shall after bring,
> Though thousand plumes she have, and thousand eies.
> Let her of *Bacchus* and *Alcides* sing,
> Of thee to future age let this suffies,
>   That of thine actes she some forewarning give,
>   Which shall in verse and noble storie live.
>   (XV, 25–26, 32)

12 Quint, pp. 180–182.

For Francis Bacon, the Pillars of Hercules were the pre-eminent symbol of the constraints which prevented the emancipation of the intellect and the assumption of power over nature. The motto of the times was to be '*Plus ultrà*, in precedence of the ancient *Non ultrà*'. He accepted the voyages of Columbus both as a symbol of the liberation of the human mind, and as an actual initiation of the new knowledge. As Wayne Franklin writes, 'The great discoverer was his hero as much as his metaphor'.[13]

The divided mind of Europe over the ethics of voyaging lies behind the divided mind of the English Renaissance writers in using the metaphor of the voyage. On the one side, there is travel as a grim token of the loss of innocence; travel undertaken because of rootlesness and restlessness; travel which further breaks down individuality, blurs distinctiveness, confuses identity; travel which would arrogantly reveal what God has chosen to conceal; travel undertaken for material gain, the enrichment of the explorer and the merchant, the lust for the gold of the west and the luxuries of the east; travel undertaken for personal glory and national ambition; travel which meant disturbing the lives of far-away peoples, corrupting their innocence, and enslaving them. On the other side, there is travel as a sign of the emancipation of mankind from darkness, of the progress of science and knowledge; travel as heroic endeavour and courageous persistence; travel as the utilization of the world's resources for the benefit of human life; travel for the increase of national standing and prosperity; travel to spread civilization and Christianity.

These oppositions create a powerful dialogue in English writing in the sixteenth and seventeenth centuries. In terms of morality and in terms of the extent of human power, the image of the voyage is not a cliché but a two-edged weapon capable of opposing what it is asked to demonstrate. Meaning is not

13 Franklin, 9.

diminished thereby, but enhanced and enriched. Voyages of discovery can become a poetics of discovery.

The opposition is not a matter of material gain versus glory. Glory and gain go together. It is the evaluation of the pair that is at issue. On the one side the gain is a material and spiritual boon, and the glory real. On the other side, the gain is greed and the glory spurious. But they are not to be separated. No gain without glory, no glory without gain. Sir Walter Ralegh wrote about his aspirations, in both a literal and a metaphoric sense, as 'to seeke new worlds, for golde, for prayse, for glory'.[14] In his ode 'To the Virginian Voyage', Michael Drayton was quite clear that both glory and gain were involved, and that both were real.

> You brave Heroique Minds,
> Worthy your Countries Name,
>   That Honour still pursue,
>   Goe, and subdue,
> Whilst loyt'ring Hinds
> Lurke here at home, with shame.
>
> .   .   .   .   .
>
> And cheerefully at Sea,
> Successe you still intice,
>   To get the Pearle and Gold
>   And ours to hold,
> VIRGINIA,
> Earth's onely Paradise.[15]

The most derisive representation of the gain-and-glory of voyaging is probably in Ben Jonson's *The Alchemist* (1610), in the character of Sir Epicure Mammon and his words to Surly at the beginning of Act II, Scene 1.

> Come on, sir. Now, you set your foot on shore
> In *novo orbe*; Here's the rich *Peru*:

14 *Ocean to Cynthia*, 61.
15 *Works*, ed. J. W. Hebel, 1932, ii, p. 363.

And there within, sir, are the golden mines,
Great SALOMON's *Ophir*! He was sayling to't
Three yeeres, but we have reach'd it in ten months.
This is the day, wherein, to all my friends,
I shall pronounce the happy word, *be rich*.

Mammon puts his expectations of riches from the fraudulent
alchemy of Subtle and Face in terms of the riches to be
expected from a project in the Americas—such as Ralegh's in
Guiana. There is much that is being devalued here. Subtle's
alchemy is a parody of Bacon's undertaking to enrich the
world by science and technology; and the expectations of *that*
fraudulent enterprise are as foolish as the dreams of riches
from oversea enterprises. The derision supplements the contempt for voyaging ventures which inspires *Eastward Ho!*, the
play written by Jonson, Marston and Chapman a few years
earlier.

The tension within the voyage metaphor is the contrary pull
between Drayton and Jonson. It is only natural that the
romance of voyaging and discovery and the allure of untold
riches at the end of a hard-fought journey to exotic places
should be employed as an image of worthwhile endeavour and
reward. But the comparison leads to endless complications.
The real voyage needs to be stripped of its very nature to
become a spiritual voyage, as we saw in Fulke Greville's poem
discussed in the Introduction. One way out of the difficulty is
not to compare but to contrast the rewards of voyaging and
devotion, as George Herbert did in one of his rare voyage-
images, in 'The Size'. He is persuading a 'greedy heart' to be
content with 'moderate joys'.

What though some have a fraught
Of cloves and nutmegs, and in cinamon sail;
If thou hast wherewithall to spice a draught,
When griefs prevail;

And for the future time art heir
To th' Isle of spices, is't not fair?[16]

The danger with this, as I argued in regard to Donne's poem
'To Mr. Tilman' (p. 73), is that a contrast is still a comparison.
The poet is ranking riches, putting heavenly reward above
earthly reward, but speaking of both in terms of material
possessions, so that they remain in the same league. The
conjunction, even though it is a contrast, adds lustre to the
merchandise, and at the same time reduces spiritual gain in the
direction of goods and chattels. The reference to 'th' Isle of
spices' risks the response of Donne's great protest: 'Is the
Pacifique Sea my home?' Gold and spices: the magic of words
in describing the riches of west and east often proves treacherous.

The description of Heaven itself in terms of gold and
precious stones is not compromised in the same way.

Then the holy paths weele travell
Strewde with Rubies thicke as gravell,
Seelings of Diamonds, Saphire floores,
High walles of Corall and Pearle Bowres.

So *The Passionate Man's Pilgrimage* ('Give me my Scallop
shell of quiet'), the recusant poem long attributed to Ralegh.[17]
All such imagery derives from Chapter XXI of the Book of
Revelation. It is particularly interesting that the riot of
jewellery there used to tell of the richness of the heavenly
Jerusalem has no difficulty in co-existing with the utter
repudiation of the riches of Babylon in Chapter XVIII, which
was sought as merchandise by sea-traders.

And the Merchants of the earth shall weepe and mourne
over her, for no man buyeth their merchandise any
more;

16 *Works*, ed. Hutchinson, Clarendon Press, 1941, p. 137.
17 *Poems*, ed. Latham (1951), p. 50.

The merchandise of gold, and silver, and pretious stones,
    and of pearles, and fine linnen . . .
The Merchants of these things which were made riche by
    her, shall stand afarre off . . .
And saying, Alas, alas, that great city, that was clothed in
    fine linnen, and purple, and scarlet, and decked with
    gold, and pretious stones, and pearles:
For in one houre so great riches is come to nought. And
    every shipmaster, and all the company in ships, and
    sailers, and as many as trade by sea, stood a farre off,
And cryed when they saw the smoke of her burning . . .

The writings of Donne are the battle-field where the conflict
between Babylon and Jerusalem is most obviously fought out.
No one is readier than Donne with the image of life as a
voyage, especially a trading voyage, in which the Christian
eventually earns the reward of his constancy and faith. The
sermons are full of the metaphor. But the metaphor is made to
seem trite and unconvincing by the challenges of Donne's own
earlier poems, in which the idea of life as a determined
progress is simply denied, being replaced by a frightening
vision of self-created frustration and paralysis. In the 'Hymne
to God my God, in my sicknesse' the idea of determined
progress implicit in the voyage image is replaced by an image
in which the sea and not the ship is the victor: the image of
drowning, when the hostile sea is miraculously changed into
the saving blood of Christ.

    It is in Marlowe's plays, however, that the mind divided
between faith in the voyage and distrust of it most sharply
shows itself. His enthusiasm for the voyage as a symbol of the
questing of the human spirit—the frail barque of the flesh
looking for infinite riches—is countered by recognition of the
self-destruction which follows the launch into the unknown.
This swinging pendulum of attraction and repulsion
accompanies another antagonism, picturing the sea both as

external danger and as self-fulfilment, which directly reflects the great travel debate.

Even Francis Bacon, the most enthusiastic and confident user of the metaphor of the voyage as a proper image for the proper life, has his hesitation. It is not explicit, but it seems to be implied in his persistence in worrying at the meaning of the legend of Hercules sailing the seas in his pitcher to rescue Prometheus. In the end, if I have read his essay on Adversity correctly, he justified the image which dominates his writings, advocating intellectual exploration and advance in terms of a voyage into unknown seas, by finding in Hercules a symbol of Christian resolution battling with hostile seas in a frail vessel to ameliorate the human condition.

Spenser seems to move his position in the debate from acceptance of voyaging to relinquishment. I argued that the sea proved too strong for the ship, and disabled the metaphor of life-as-a-voyage. It is not Guyon, buoyant on the waves, but Calidore, resting from his voyage among the shepherds, who dominates the later stages of *The Faerie Queene*. There must have been something in the spirit of the times pushing Spenser in his enthusiasm for voyaging as a metaphor at the start of his epic. The decay of that enthusiasm surely marks a radical change in his view of life, wholly unadmitted, even to himself.

Milton's voyage imagery was deeply influenced by his opposition to colonialism. Though he is writing at the end of our time span from the 1580s to the 1660s, he is in spirit quite firmly with Calidore. The voyage is always associated with the fallen state of mankind, a restless seeking and searching quite foreign to the life of Eden or Heaven. Real voyages in pursuit of riches and territory were both symbols and examples of the nature of human life as it ought not to be but had to be. Milton stands at the opposite extreme from Bacon in his attitude to voyaging and his use of it as metaphor. But, as with Bacon, the issue is not clear-cut. The night-time in which his voyage similes usually operate is lightened by a pervading compassion for those who have no choice but to 'wander in that perilous flood'.

Where does Shakespeare stand in this dialectic of voyaging? I argued that in spite of the profound engagement of his writings in issues of nation and empire, in his voyage meta-phors he was not taking sides in the long debate on the ethics of travel. In that passage of *The Enchafed Flood* mentioned above, Auden suggested that in *The Winter's Tale* the words of Camillo advising Florizel and Perdita 'to enlist the help of Leontes rather than to elope' were evidence of the older attitude to voyaging as unnatural and illegitimate.

> A Course more promising,
> Then a wild dedication of your selves
> To unpath'd Waters, undream'd Shores; most certaine,
> To Miseries enough . . .
>
> (4. 4. 565–68)

But after all, Camillo is trying to alarm Florizel with this frightening prospect as part of his strategy to get them and him to Sicily. It is a strong vision of remote navigations, and it arises from contemporary voyages of discovery, but it doesn't unsettle the general neutrality of Shakespeare's voyage meta-phors.

Nevertheless, it is left to Shakespeare to bring forward the one resounding affirmation of life as a providential voyage, in which all mishaps, setbacks, and disasters are subsumed within the overall guidance of watchful Providence. This is what we have been looking for in the pro-travel side of the scales—the parallel in imaginative literature of what was so often and so forcefully expressed in polemical prose by Hakluyt and others, namely the idea that God was helping England to work out its destiny as an imperial power in the New World, and that every voyage was playing its part in the fulfilment of a divinely ordained future. At the end of *The Tempest* Gonzalo sees the extraordinary adventures of their voyage to and from Tunis as evidence of divine direction and protection.

> Looke downe you gods
> And on this couple drop a blessed crowne;
> For it is you, that have chalk'd forth the way
> Which brought us hither . . .
> Was *Millaine* thrust from *Millaine*, that his Issue
> Should become Kings of *Naples*? O rejoyce
> Beyond a common joy, and set it downe
> With gold on lasting Pillers: In one voyage
> Did *Claribell* her husband finde at *Tunis*,
> And *Ferdinand* her brother, found a wife,
> Where he himselfe was lost: *Prospero* his Dukedome
> In a poore Isle: and all of us, our selves,
> When no man was his owne.

How do we respond to Gonzalo's enthusiasm? The dominating voyage-image in Shakespeare is not that of the weather-beaten ship arriving safely in harbour, but the shipwreck, implicit in the tragedies, of which it is the termination, and explicit in the comedies and romances, of which it is the commencement. Othello looks back over the trackless waters and sees his life as a course set towards the sea-mark of destruction. Like Macbeth, he views his navigation as something shared with deflecting supernatural forces—for him the demi-devil Iago, for Macbeth the witches. As the Chorus said (concerning Dalila) in *Samson Agonistes:*

> What Pilot so expert but needs must wreck
> Imbarkt with such a Stears-mate at the Helm?

The play of *Macbeth* has throughout implied that navigation is a fundamental image of life—so fundamental that Macbeth appeals to it as one of the essentials of existence even as he is perverting it—with the concept of drifting as the destabilizing and distorting of society by malignant force. It can be argued that this image of navigation, never developed in the play, at least suggests a suppressed image of the providential voyage, and such a view of the play would be in line with Macduff's exultation over 'this dead Butcher, and his Fiend-like Queene'. 'The time is free', he says. The ship of state is free to resume its proper course. But *Macbeth*, like all the other tragedies, contains no overt acceptance of the idea of divine planning and divine control. If the last word is with Macduff, it is spoken over the echoing words of Macbeth, that life is a tale told by an idiot, signifying nothing—a directionless ship, drifting. To compare a small work with a great one, Macbeth's words act like Wyatt's refrain, *'en vogant la galère'*, to question faith in life as purposeful navigation (see pp. 10–12).

The play of *King Lear* makes a point of not accepting the confidence of the *dramatis personae* in the presence of God in every event, and His long-term protection of those who profess their belief in Him. The 'degree' speech of Ulysses in *Troilus and Cressida*, with its affirmation of cosmic order, is more certainly the voice of Ulysses than it is the voice of Shakespeare. Gonzalo's speech is more than a personal view, and it differs from speeches by Albany or Ulysses in being an important contribution to the final mood of the play. But its context confines it to the world of the play, and challenges its general applicability.

With the shipwrecks that so often initiate the comedies we enter into a kind of fantasy replay of life as it might have been or might be, cancelling out disaster and rebuilding a future that has greater consonance with our desires. Shakespeare constantly emphasizes the theatricality of it all: if we are taken in he is not. The strongest mark of this theatricality is in the many signs of divine intervention in the Romances—what Wilson Knight called 'theophanies'. Jupiter's descent on an eagle in *Cymbeline*, the restoration of Hermione in *The Winter's Tale*, the arraignment of the 'three men of sinne' by the 'ministers of Fate' in *The Tempest*—all these are shows, with their theatricality calling attention to itself. Whatever confidence Shakespeare might privately have had in the benignity and protectiveness of divine powers, assurance in his comedies and romances is offered as therapy rather than theology. The providential voyage ends in the theatre. In any case, it is impossible to see the fable of the voyage in *The Tempest* as an endorsement of England's imperial future. The Europeans go back home and leave Caliban to himself on the island.

The special vitality of the voyage metaphor between Spenser and Milton is in the equivocation of its message. In one final respect its power both to affirm and to refute has an ironic resemblance to reality. Like voyaging, writing can be the laborious fulfilment of ambitious purpose; the powerful presence of the voyager in the imagination of Tudor and Stuart writers shows itself in the identification of themselves as voyagers and their work as a voyage. Edmund Spenser and Francis Bacon were the literary voyagers-in-chief. They wrote under the banner which Ben Jonson chose for himself from Seneca: 'Tanquam explorator'.[18] Each set off confidently on a major voyage; if the seas were largely uncharted the course was declared and the destination announced. For each, an uncompleted magnum opus, *The Faerie Queene* and the *Instauratio Magna*, remains as a potent sign of the infirmity of human resolution, and the frequent fate of the aspiring voyager to whom they have so often compared themselves. Humphrey Gilbert, Henry Hudson, Sir Walter Ralegh all gave themselves projects on the terrestrial globe as huge and uncertain as those that Spenser and Bacon gave themselves in writing, and not one of them achieved his objective. Ralegh of course also had his own massive literary project in *The History of the World*, something to set beside *The Faerie Queene* and *Instauratio Magna*, begun when he was a prisoner in the

18 Jonson appropriately enough was not thinking of himself as an intrepid seaman, but as a searcher or seeker-out of ideas. See *Ben Jonson*, ed. Herford and Simpson, i, p. 261.

Tower under sentence of death, a work uncompleted and uncompletable—as if at dusk—

> Wee should beginn by such a partinge light
> To write the story of all ages past
> And end the same before th' approchinge night.[19]

Ralegh was unusual in being a voyager both figuratively and in reality. The disaster of his final expedition shows us all too clearly why in literature the voyage stands out as an emblem of uncertainty.

19 Ralegh, *Ocean to Cynthia*, 101–03.

REFERENCES

Adamson   Jane Adamson. *'Othello' as Tragedy: Some Problems of Judgment and Feeling*. Cambridge: Cambridge University Press, 1980.

Bethell   S. L. Bethell. 'Shakespeare's Imagery: The Diabolic Images in *Othello*', *Shakespeare Survey*, 5 (1952), pp. 62–80.

Broaddus   James W. Broaddus. *Spenser's Allegory of Love: Social Vision in Books III, IV, and V of 'The Faerie Queene'*. London: Associated University Presses, 1995.

Bullough   Geoffrey Bullough (ed.). *Narrative and Dramatic Sources of Shakespeare*. London: Routledge and Kegan Paul; New York: Columbia University Press. 8 vols, 1957–75.

Carey   John Carey. *John Donne: Life, Mind and Art*. London: Faber and Faber, 1981; new edition, 1990.

Cawley   Robert Rawston Cawley. *Unpathed Waters: Studies in the Influence of the Voyagers on Elizabethan Literature*. Princeton: Princeton University Press, 1940.

Davies   Stevie Davies. *Milton*. Harvester New Readings. Hemel Hempstead, Hertfordshire: Harvester Wheatsheaf, 1991.

Dees   Jerome S. Dees. 'The Ship Conceit in *The Faerie Queene*: "Conspicuous Allusion" and Poetic Structure', *Studies in Philology*, 72 (1975) pp. 208–225.

Edwards (1986)   Philip Edwards. 'Tragic Balance in *Hamlet*', in *Shakespeare Survey*, 36 (1986), pp. 43–52.

Edwards (1988)   Philip Edwards. *Last Voyages: Cavendish, Hudson, Ralegh. The Original Narratives*. Oxford: Clarendon Press, 1988.

Edwards (1990)   Philip Edwards. "Thrusting Elysium into Hell: The Originality of *The Spanish Tragedy*', in *The Elizabethan Theatre XI*, ed. A.L.Magnusson and C. E. McGee. Port Credit, Ont.: P. D. Meany, 1990.

Edwards (1992)   Philip Edwards. 'Edward Hayes explains away Sir Humphrey Gilbert', *Renaissance Studies*, 8 (1992), pp. 270–86.

Edwards (1994)   Philip Edwards. *The Story of the Voyage: Sea-*

narratives in eighteenth-century England. Cambridge: Cambridge University Press, 1994.

Edwards (1996) Philip Edwards. 'Tragic Form and the Voyagers', in *Travel and Drama in Shakespeare's Time*, ed. J. P. Maquerlot and M. Willems. Cambridge: Cambridge University Press, 1996.

Empson William Empson. 'Honest in Othello', in *The Structure of Complex Words.* London: Chatto and Windus, 1951.

Evans J. Martin Evans (ed.). John Milton, *Paradise Lost, Books IX–X*. Cambridge: Cambridge University Press, 1973.

Fish Stanley Fish. *Self-Consuming Artifacts.* Berkeley, Los Angeles, London: University of California Press, 1972.

Fletcher Angus Fletcher. *The Prophetic Moment: An Essay on Spenser.* Chicago and London: University of Chicago Press, 1971.

Fowler Alastair Fowler (ed.). *Paradise Lost*, in *The Poems of John Milton*, ed. John Carey and Alastair Fowler. London: Longmans, 1968.

Franklin Wayne Franklin. *Discoverers, Explorers, Settlers: The Diligent Writers of Early America.* Chicago: University of Chicago Press, 1979.

Gillies John Gillies. *Shakespeare and the Geography of Difference.* Cambridge: Cambridge University Press, 1994.

Greenblatt Stephen Greenblatt. *Renaissance Self-Fashioning: From More to Shakespeare.* Chicago and London: Chicago University Press, 1980.

Greene Thomas Greene. *The Descent from Heaven: A Study in Epic Continuity.* New Haven and London: Yale University Press, 1963.

Grene Nicholas Grene. *Shakespeare's Tragic Imagination.* London: Macmillan, 1992.

Hakluyt Richard Hakluyt. *The Principal Navigations, Voyages, Traffiques and Discoveries of the English Nation* (1598–1600). Glasgow: MacLehose, 1903–1905. Reprinted, New York, 1969.

Hamilton A. C. Hamilton (general editor). *The Spenser Encyclopedia.* Toronto and Buffalo: University of Toronto Press; London: Routledge, 1990.

Heilman Robert B. Heilman. *Magic in the Web: Action and Language in 'Othello'.* Lexington: University of Kentucky Press, 1956.

Hill   Christopher Hill. *Milton and the English Revolution.* London: Faber and Faber, 1977.

Hough   Graham Hough. *A Preface to 'The Faerie Queeene'.* London: Duckworth, 1962.

Hunt   Clay Hunt. *Donne's Poetry: Essays in Literary Analysis.* New Haven: Yale University Press, 1954.

Hunter   G. K. Hunter. *Dramatic Identities and Cultural Tradition: Studies in Shakespeare and his Contemporaries.* Liverpool: Liverpool University Press, 1978.

Jardine   Lisa Jardine. *Francis Bacon: Discovery and the Art of Discourse.* Cambridge: Cambridge University Press, 1974.

Johnson   Francis R. Johnson. *Astronomical Thought in Renaissance England.* Baltimore: Johns Hopkins Press, 1937. Reprinted New York: Octagon Books, 1968.

Knight (1930)   George Wilson Knight. 'The *Othello* Music', in *The Wheel of Fire.* London: Oxford University Press, 1930; London: Methuen, 1965.

Knight (1932)   George Wilson Knight. *The Shakespearian Tempest.* (1932.) Reissued London: Oxford University Press, 1940.

Knight (1947)   George Wilson Knight. *The Crown of Life. Essays in Interpretation of Shakespeare's Final Plays.* London: Oxford University Press, 1947.

Leavis   F. R. Leavis. 'Diabolic Intellect and the Noble Hero: or The Sentimentalist's Othello'. In *The Common Pursuit.* (London: Chatto and Windus, 1952; Harmondsworth: Penguin Books), 1962. pp. 136–69.

Lein   Clayton D. Lein. 'Donne's "The Storme: The Poem and the Tradition.' *English Literary Renaissance*, 4 (1974), pp. 137–63.

Lewalski   Barbara Lewalski. 'The Ship-Tempest Imagery in *Samson Agonistes'. Notes and Queries*, 6 (1959), pp. 372–73.

Lewis   C. S. Lewis. *The Allegory of Love: A Sudy in Medieval Tradition.* Oxford: Oxford University Press, (1936) 1970.

Lovejoy and Boas   A. O. Lovejoy and George Boas. *Primitivism and Related Ideas in Antiquity.* Baltimore: The Johns Hopkins Press, 1935.

MacCaffrey (1967)   Isabel G. MacCaffrey. *'Paradise Lost' as 'Myth'.* Cambridge. Mass.: Harvard University Press, 1967.

MacCaffrey (1975)   Robert Hodge and Isabel G. MacCaffrey (ed.). John Milton, *Paradise Lost, Books V–VI*. Cambridge: Cambridge University Press, 1975.

MacCaffrey (1976)   Isabel G. MacCaffrey. *Spenser's Allegory: The Anatomy of Imagination*. Princeton, N.J.: Princeton University Press, 1976.

McElroy   Bernard McElroy. *Shakespeare's Mature Tragedies*. Princeton, N.J.: Princeton University Press, 1973.

Marienstras   Richard Marienstras. *New Perspectives on the Shakespearian World* (1981). Trans. Janet Lloyd. Cambridge: Cambridge University Press, 1985.

Mizejewski   Linda Mizejewski. 'Darkness and Disproportion: A Study of Donne's "Storme" and "Calme" ', *JEGP*, 76, 1977, pp. 217–30.

Muir   Kenneth Muir. *The Sources of Shakespeare's Plays*. London: Methuen, 1977.

Nellist (1963)   Brian Nellist. 'The Allegory of Guyon's Voyage: An Interpretation.' *ELH*, 30 (1963), pp. 89–106. Reprinted in *Critical Essays on Spenser from ELH*. Baltimore and London: Johns Hopkins Press, 1970, pp. 188–205.

Nellist (1964)   Brian Nellist. 'Donne's "Storm" and "Calm" and the Descriptive Tradition', *Modern Language Review*, 59 (1964), pp. 511–15.

Nellist (1974)   Brian Nellist (ed.). John Milton. *Poems of 1645 and Comus*. London and Glasgow: Collins, 1974.

Pagden   Anthony Pagden. *European Encounters with the New World: From Renaissance to Romanticism*. New Haven and London: Yale University Press, 1993.

Parker   Patricia A. Parker. *Inescapable Romance: Studies in the Poetics of a Mode*. Princeton, N.J.: Princeton University Press, 1979.

Peterson   Richard S. Peterson. *Imitation and Praise in the Poems of Ben Jonson*. New Haven and London: Yale University Press, 1981.

Quint   David Quint. 'The Boat of Romance and Renaissance Epic', In *Romance: Generic Transformation from Chrétien de Troyes to Cervantes*. Ed. Kevin Brownlee and Marina S. Brownlee. Hanover, N.H.: University Press of New England, 1985.

Rajan   Balachandra Rajan. *The Form of the Unfinished: English*

Poetics from Spenser to Pound. Princeton, N.J.: Princeton University Press, 1985.

Rennie Neil Rennie. *Far-Fetched Facts: The Literature of Travel and the Idea of the South Seas*. Oxford: Clarendon Press, 1995.

Roche Thomas P. Roche, Jr. *The Kindly Flame: A Study of the Third and Fourth Books of Spenser's 'Faerie Queene'*. Princeton, N.J.: Princeton University Press, 1964.

Rugoff Milton A. Rugoff. *Donne's Imagery: A Study in Creative Sources* (1939). Repr. New York: Russell and Russell, 1962.

Shirley John W. Shirley (ed.). *Thomas Harriot: Renaissance Scientist*. Oxford: Clarendon Press, 1974.

Stewart J. I. M.Stewart. *Character and Motive in Shakespeare*. London: Longmans, Green, 1949.

Vickers Brian Vickers. *Francis Bacon and Renaissance Prose*. Cambridge: Cambridge University Press, 1968.

Waller Gary Waller. *Edmund Spenser: A Literary Life*. Basingstoke: Macmillan, 1994.

Whitney Charles Whitney. *Francis Bacon and Modernity*. New Haven and London: Yale University Press, 1986.

Williams (1966) Kathleen Williams. *Spenser's 'Faerie Queene': The World of Glass*. London: Routledge & Kegan Paul, 1966.

Williams (1970–71) Kathleen Williams. 'Spenser: Some Uses of the Sea and the Storm-tossed Ship', *Research Opportunities in Renaissance Drama*, 13–14 (1970–71), pp. 135–42.

Yeats W. B. Yeats. *Essays and Introductions*. London: Macmillan, 1961.

INDEX

223

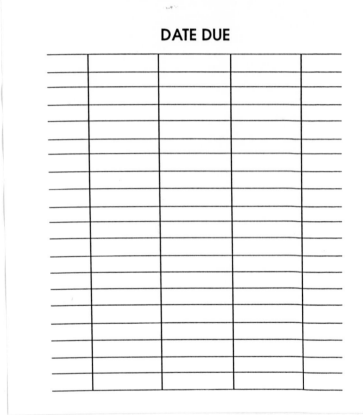

DATE DUE